Rick Mather: Urban Approaches

TO TOMY WITH THANKS FOR
THE HELP Rick 16 APRIL 1993
LONDON

Hugh Pearman   with foreword by Alan Colquhoun

RICK MATHER:
URBAN APPROACHES

Rick Mather:
Urban Approaches

First published in
Great Britain in 1992 by
Fourth Estate Ltd,
289 Westbourne Grove,
London W11 2QA
in conjunction with
Blueprint magazine,
26 Cramer Street,
London W1M 3HE

A catalogue record for this
book is available from the
British Library

ISBN 1 85702 007 3

Series editor:
Arthur Valenzuela
Cover photograph:
Phil Sayer
Design: Peter Brawne
Production: Spy Graphics
Colour reproduction:
Fotographics Ltd,
UK/Hong Kong
Printed and bound
in Hong Kong

Photographic credits

Michael Boys 14.
Richard Bryant/Arcaid
26, 42, 43, 64, 67, 68,
69, 70/71, 72, 73, 74/75, 76,
79, 84 (top).
Martin Charles 84 (bottom).
Jake Chessum 2.
Peter Cook 87, 94, 95,
97, 106, 107.
Andre Cornellier 82, 83.
Richard Davies 34, 35.
John Donat 44, 55, 57, 60.
Chris Gascoine 109.
Denis Gilbert 88, 90/91,
101.
Ian Lambot/Arcaid 78.
Allan Mower 11.
Murphy & Hershman 46,
48, 49, 50, 51.
Paul Raftery 99, 103.
Sealand Aerial
Photography 53.
Ken Tam 31, 37, 39.

Acknowledgements

My thanks to Anne French,
lately of Rick Mather's
office, and to Ian Hay and
Aya Ruppin, for their help
in the research of this book

Blueprint Monographs

Ron Arad: Restless Furniture
Deyan Sudjic

Nigel Coates:
The City in Motion
Rick Poynor

Rei Kawakubo and
Comme des Garçons
Deyan Sudjic

Eva Jiricna: Design in Exile
Martin Pawley

King and Miranda:
The Poetry of the Machine
Hugh Aldersey-Williams

Javier Mariscal:
Designing the New Spain
Emma Dent Coad

Queensberry Hunt:
Creativity and Industry
Susannah Walker

Rodney Kinsman:
The Logical Art of Furniture
Jose Manser

Stansted: Norman Foster and
the Architecture of Flight
Kenneth Powell

Contents

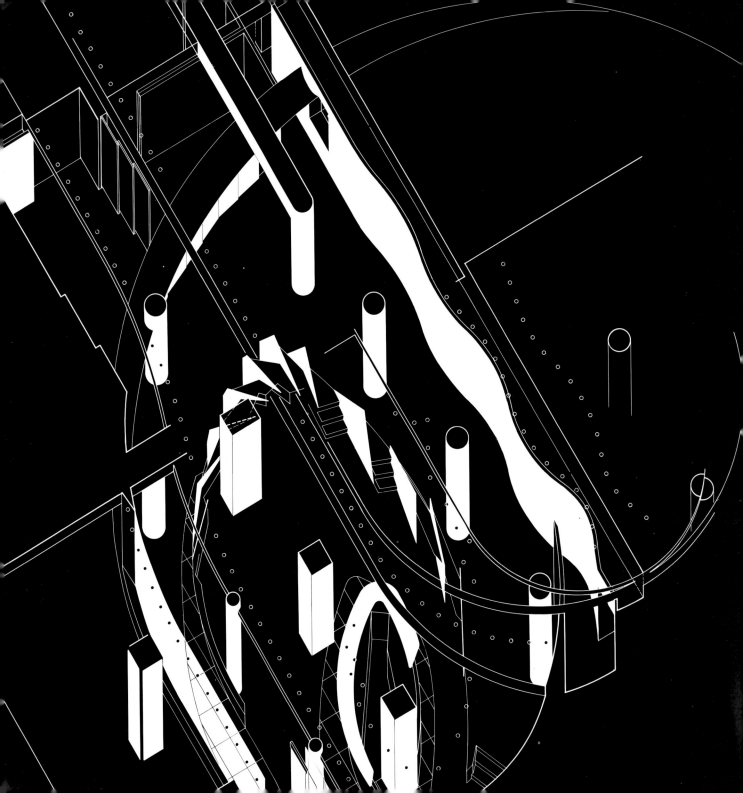

To give an adequate account of the work of Rick Mather it is essential to look briefly at the state of architecture, both in England and internationally, so as to be able to place his work in context.

The present situation is not easy to define. After two decades in which the most interesting work often reflected clearly defined theoretical positions, we find ourselves in a situation characterised by a great variety of tendencies, which either lack any explicit theoretical framework, or are backed up more by dogmatic assertion than by argument. The most obvious fact about the present situation is that, following the critical decline of Postmodernism, there has been a resurgence of the Modernist tradition. But how can we define this tradition today? It has seventy years of development behind it, with its various early sub-movements – Rationalism, Purism, Expressionism, Constructivism, Organicism – available as paradigms. It is interpreted differently in different countries, by different architects, and accordingly to different theoretical models, where such models exist and, conversely, it is subject to the instantaneous transmissions of fashion in a critical ambience dominated by the media. Given these facts, and the analyses of the (Post)Modern condition offered by theorists like Jean-François Lyotard and Gianni Vattimo, it is difficult to sustain the totalising claims originally made for Modernism.

Two tendencies stand out from this confused picture. The first is characterised by a radicalism that sees architecture as an aspect of a more general cultural crisis – as a critical discourse whose task is to question all existing values by a process of systematic negation. Although this attitude seems to be a distillation of the millennialist tendencies of the historical avant-gardes, it is often claimed that it is an essentially Postmodern phenomenon, since it rejects the humanistic assumptions and aspirations that were retained by high Modernism. The second tendency, popularly known as "High Tech", is characteristic of much work in England, and, rather less exclusively, elsewhere in Europe. It lays claim to the unproblematic high ground of modernity, converting current technology into a high art style. These two positions sometimes overlap, when "irrational" forms, originally carrying subversive connotations, are appropriated for the market. Indeed, it is a feature of High Tech that it adapted very efficiently to the demands of the 1980s consumer boom and that it is often supported by a style of criticism more reminiscent of the fashion magazine than the old-style professional journal.

A large amount of work, however, falls outside these categories, and this is far more complex and difficult to define. One reason for this is that it tends to avoid doctrinaire, totalising theories and to occupy, more modestly, the borderlines between conflicting pressures. The work of Rick Mather belongs to this broad category. Though it undoubtedly shows certain affinities with High Tech, particularly in its lightness and transparency and in its preference for synthetic, hard, machine-worked materials, it does not lend itself to simple classification and always remains sensitive to the context and the specifics of the programme. In its professionalism and in the way it seeks to synthesise multiple and sometimes contradictory aspects of the Modernist tradition, it has affinities with a growing body of work in Europe.

Mather himself has set out some of the principles informing his work. In a talk at the RIBA in 1984 he spoke of his refusal to accept either revivalism or technology as the primary generators of form and of his belief in the simultaneous need for the ideal and for its contamination by programme and context. In saying this, Mather revealed himself to be a dualist who seeks to avoid the false simplicities of both idealism and empiricism. In the same lecture he defined "context" as consisting, first and foremost, of the city. More specifically, it was the London of Steen Eiler Rasmussen's great book – the residential London of Georgian terraces and squares and their Victorian extensions. It is obvious from Mather's work that his concept of the city does not imply the imitation and reproduction of its traditional forms. Rather it implies the city as the existing environment with which modern works have to enter into a dialogue.

In interpreting Mather's highly nuanced position it is important to realise that his formation is American rather than English. He received his professional training at the University of Oregon, where his teachers were, among others, Lee Hodgden and Alvin Boyarsky, and where his fellow students included Fred Koetter and Michael Dennis. It is always difficult to measure the influence exerted by, or on, teachers and colleagues, but to mention these names is at once to suggest an atmosphere very different from that of a typical English school in the late 1950s, with its empirical and social biases. In America, partly owing to the continuing influence of the Beaux Arts, Modernism was tied back to the architectural tradition by formal principles which could be "taught", and which seemed especially evident in the work of Le Corbusier, de Stijl and, to a lesser extent, Aalto. This formalist tradition, which had more in common with certain countries of continental Europe than with England, has been largely responsible for the principal tendencies of the American neo-avant-garde since the early 1970s – from the New York Five, to Venturi and the more recent forms of abstract Postmodernism and Deconstructivism.

But although his work is strongly marked by this background, Mather seems to have welcomed in England a degree of social commitment that was lacking in America, and to have felt the need to test his formal research against social reality and a tightly knit urban public realm. His response to context is seen in two very different types of project. The first is chiefly concerned with interior space and its ornamental elaboration. It takes the form of single-cell volumes carved out of the existing urban fabric, and its main example is a series of restaurants – four in London, one in Hong Kong and one in Montreal – built in the last five years. The fact that all these commissions have the same client has enabled him to treat them as a continuous research project and to refine and develop their formal and spatial language. In most of these projects, Mather's skill in the use of glass has led to a dematerialisation of the front wall so that the new volume becomes a visual extension of the pavement. The first example of this treatment was a bookshop in Holland Park designed in 1974, but its most striking is his latest restaurant, located in the heart of London's West End, where not only has the space been turned inside out, so that the restaurant becomes like a stage with its missing fourth wall, but vertical continuity has been created between three floors, including a basement made transparent to the street by means of glass paving. The "vanishing" glass wall plays a somewhat ambiguous role, connecting the restaurant visually to the outside, but rendering it mute and untouchable at the same time. This effect has more to do with contemporary media culture with its stress on the visual, and its blurring of the distinctions between "reality" and semblance, than it has to do with the Parisian sidewalk café.

In this project, as in his other restaurants, Mather indulges in visual puns, like the ceiling lights which pick out the constellation "Orion" in a discreet reference to the new name of the refurbished host building. But such games are played in the context of a carefully worked out formal decorative system consisting of either quasi-structural ornaments, like the spectacular bucket fountain that swoops down through successive floor voids, or the use of reflecting or transparent materials, particularly stainless steel and glass in all its forms (clear, frosted, etched, mirrored). This form of decoration has its distant ancestor in Adolf Loos, who used the sensuous surface qualities of materials to create an effect of luxury that no longer had to depend on handicraft. The use of machine-worked products as decoration (often in a form very remote from that of Loos) has been a feature of a school of shop and restaurant interior design that emerged in the 1980s and Mather's restaurant work belongs to this trend, even if his earliest interior work pre-dates it by several years. There has, in fact, been a slight but noticeable shift in his treatment of metal furniture (particularly chairs and balustrades) away from the earlier forms recalling the classicism of the 1920s, towards greater lightness, tensility and geometrical complexity, reflecting current Constructivist enthusiasms. But this interest in lattice-like structure is always balanced by a strong formal control – even by a certain minimalism – and Mather's work completely avoids the fetishistic ornamentalism that spoils many recent "High Tech" shop interiors in London.

Mather's interiors are able to concentrate on the more evanescent, delicate and transparent aspects of the Modernist tradition because a complimentary density of meaning is provided by the city fabric in which they are inserted. But when he designs complete structures, he starts from the opposite premise. The building acts as its own context, generating an internal dialogue between its parts, while at the same time instituting a dialogue with its context. This double process can be seen in his major on-going commission, the extensions to the University of East Anglia in Norwich.

Denys Lasdun's original scheme, designed in the 1960s took the form of a continuous megastructure containing the seed of its own extension. The theoretical model on which this scheme was based was the idea of the university as a microcosm of, and paradigm for, the collective society. As a totalising vision of both society and

From the left: two stools in chrome-plated steel tube and leather designed for the AA bar (1978); chair and stool designed for Now and Zen (1990); stainless steel rod and leather chair for Zen Hong Kong (1988)

architecture, this model may be outdated, but Lasdun's complex remains a strong, coherent statement and, unlike Norman Foster in his Sainsbury Centre, Mather has seen it as something to respect and to respond to in a positive way. In the first phase of his extension he solved this problem by developing new structures as foils to the continuous wall of the original project. He made no attempt to relate his new buildings stylistically to the old. In contrast to Lasdun's schematically emphasised, béton brut floor slabs which stress the depth the building rather than its surface, Mather's two buildings – a cylinder and a three-sided court building – are presented as static, geometrical forms, sheathed in white glazed blocks.

In the student residences proposed for the second phase, a somewhat different strategy has been adopted. Two isolated buildings are added to either end of the campus, one serpentine in plan, the other consisting of straight, articulated slabs. Both these groups of buildings respect the linear forms of the original design but, again, neither make any attempt to continue Lasdun's unitary concept. They are buildings in their own right with their own character – a character which pays homage to tradition in its tripartite division of the façade into base, piano nobile and roof.

Significantly, the new residences are not developed as rooms strung out horizontally, as in the original scheme, but are grouped in vertical "houses", making a change from an abstract notion of community (*Gesellschaft*) to a concrete one (*Gemeinschaft*) which simulates the nuclear family. However, a corresponding change has not occurred in the buildings' external form. Each group is seen as an architectural unity, emphasised by a widely projecting flat roof, and is only broken, by means of sculpturally eroded corners, at the points of collective entry. This lack of fit between form and content is a further example of Mather's break with orthodoxies of Modernism.

One further example will suffice to illustrate Mather's dialectical approach: the new office building near Tower Bridge in London.

Again we find an initial social response to the programme, in his "green" resistance to the normal commercial strategy of deep, artificially ventilated work space. In this building the office floors are sufficiently shallow to allow for natural ventilation and good natural light (although air-conditioning has, in the end, been added). The building spans between two streets, with a long entrance lobby that takes exciting advantage of a storey's height difference between front and back. Its long, main façade is flanked by existing brick structures, and the building responds to these by means of a tripartite vertical sub-division whose outer sections are clad in brick and whose central section is fully glazed and given depth by means of external galleries. The role of "portico" given to this central part is clear and is underlined by pulling out the central bays of the concrete frame. Mather, however, immediately undermines this impression by making the porch gradually disappear into the brick fabric at one end. This odd effect is the consequence of the superimposition of two solutions – one "ideal", the other empirical – to the problem posed by a slightly irregular site boundary. Typically, Mather has thematised this "problem", rather than hiding it. Typical, also, of his love of allusion, is the reference to Edward D Stone's Museum of Modern Art façade in the punctured canopy at roof level – a device which further enhances the "receiving" quality of the central bay.

In analysing some typical examples of Rick Mather's work, I have tried to show that its virtues lie in the way it accepts the complexity of the architectural problem in present-day conditions and expresses this in a technique of design that might be called (to borrow rather freely Mikhail Bakhtin's theory of the novel) "dialogical". Mather's work is Modernist, but it is a Post-Postmodern Modernism shot through with references, allusions and compositional devices. It is practical and serious in its response to the technical and social aspects of the architectural programme, but this pragmatism is used to increase rather than diminish the works' aesthetic interest. Ideality is suggested, not an ideal world.

Chapter one

MOVING TO THE METROPOLIS

Rick Mather, Oregon-born and trained, left the States and came to London in 1963. Ten years later, he set up his own practice. By the 1990s, he had clearly arrived. Rick Mather Architects had acquired a distinctive voice of its own to become a force in the land.

After the years of learning, of teaching, of converting houses and of designing restaurants, Mather was handling large-scale urban projects with confidence and the backing of a large office. It had been a long, gradual climb from being an architect's architect to being a public architect. But more to the point, Mather had become the Londoner par excellence in the intervening years.

There was never any doubt, though, about Mather's chosen vocation. Born in Portland, Oregon in 1937, he was educated in schools around the Western states, corresponding to the career moves made by his father, an electrical engineer. He is emphatic that he never wanted to be anything other than an architect. To which end, the architecture school at Oregon in the 1950s was a good place to be.

Back in the 1930s, Oregon had been one of the first architecture schools in the US to reject the Beaux-Arts control from Paris and teach modern architecture. Its library shelves were well stocked not only with standard works, but with books and magazines from the early days of the architectural revolution.

Mather's major influences at this stage were, however, historical. His second-year design tutor, Earl Moursund, introduced him to Camillo Sitte's *The Art of Building a City* – the influential view from late nineteenth-century Vienna of what makes the medieval centres of European cities work, in terms of buildings and the outdoor spaces they define. Meanwhile, Marion Ross, Mather's history teacher, had given him a stack of *Baedeker's Guides to Europe* to read.

Latin American architecture also interested Mather for a while, to the extent that he took a year's extra course in the subject at Oregon. But Europe as a destination gradually became inevitable for a variety of reasons. One was the arrival at Oregon, in Mather's fifth year, of an ambitious new tutor, Alvin Boyarsky. Mather compares his arrival with that of a Roman grandee visiting the far-flung reaches of empire: for Boyarsky, with his Canadian roots and English wife, Liz, had the cosmopolitan air of one who served architecture in Montreal, London and Cornell. He was, temperamentally, an East-Coaster, managing to imply that the East Coast was effortlessly superior to the West, and that Europe (where he had worked with Yorke Rosenberg and Mardall) was in turn superior to North America. However, Boyarsky admired the vernacular timber buildings to be found scattered throughout the forests of Oregon, a building form that was already appreciated by the school in general and by Mather in particular. Mather had just returned from a summer tour of Europe, where he had visited folk museums in Norway and Denmark to study the origins of the Oregon timber vernacular style – in particular the European medieval barn, which in plan and section is near-identical to its Western States counterpart. Mather took the line, he recalls, that he needed no lessons in European sophistication from Boyarsky. But the older man reinforced his own opinion that Europe offered the kind of urban opportunities Mather was after.

Boyarsky stayed on at Oregon for a few years after Mather left. The two were to meet periodically thereafter and when Boyarsky, after the usual controversy that attended his movements, finally became head of the Architectural Association school in London, Mather found himself not just teaching at the AA but later, at the invitation of the AA Council, redesigning its premises as well.

After that first trip to Europe in 1959, two commissions were occupying Mather. Both were for houses in the Oregon forests: the first, in the time-honoured tradition of architects starting their careers, was for his aunt and uncle. Set on a wooded hillside looking out over Ashland, in the south of the state, it was a two-storey timber house, square in plan, at a time when most new dwellings in the area were in single-storey ranch style. Mather put the bedrooms downstairs and the living-room upstairs, so as to make the most of the view without having to cut down the manzanita and pine trees in front of the house. A bridge linked the upper floor back to the hillside and a carport behind, and a two-storey volume containing a staircase linked down to the ground-floor entrance. This early experiment in upside-down living was later to be refined extensively in Mather's work in London.

The second house, for a university friend's brother, was another setting worthy of *Walden* in a forest valley next to a stream. For this non-traditional building, Mather used traditional materials: it was a 27-foot cube, flat-roofed, and three storeys high. More than merely an exercise in symmetry for its own sake, the idea here was to achieve the greatest volume within the least external surface by means of the simplest possible structural system: four posts and the external wall provided all the vertical support.

Working for his family, says Mather, taught him never to shrink from suggesting an opportunity to a client just because the budget seems to rule it out. In this case, knowing the cost constraints, Mather built a typical Oregon cedar deck off the top living-room storey only, not daring to suggest that a second deck off the ground-floor bedrooms beneath might be twice as nice. The house complete, one of his aunt's architecture-minded friends came round and pointed out the missed opportunity. His aunt demanded to know why he hadn't thought of it. The truth was, he had thought of it too much.

Oregon, though, could not hold Mather's attention for long. The first house was completed after Mather left university while he was away for six months in the army: it acquired a pitched roof in his absence. The second was built slowly by its owner, which meant that it was finished only after its author had graduated and left for good. In the country he was to adopt, students seldom get a chance to do a whole house, let alone two. But a different situation prevailed in his home state. "These were passing things," he comments now, "You get these opportunities if you live in Oregon – everyone's building a little house somewhere. There was less planning control then, so you could build almost anything, anywhere." It was not that it wasn't real architecture: more that the context was not demanding enough. What drew Mather to Europe,

In these early conceptual sketches for Espoo, major work destinations are placed at opposite ends of town to reduce rush hour traffic. Footpaths (dotted lines) run through the central park to the bay and lake at either end. Bus routes (dashed lines) run through the residential areas and road traffic is kept to the perimeter

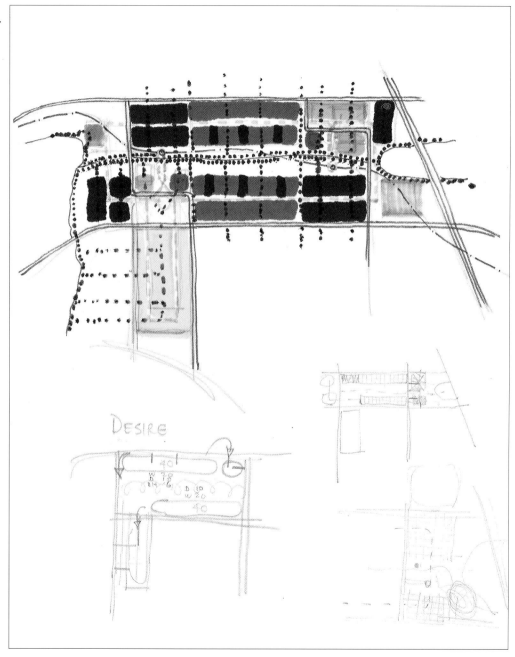

and to England, was the grain and intensity of cities that were only too demanding.

His last American commission before heading for England was to convert a terraced house for his parents in Washington DC. His father was working there on a project initiated by the Kennedy administration to design and develop a national high-voltage power grid. The house conversion was no more than a modest tuning up of a three-storey turn-of-the-century house, replanning the ground floor and redoing the kitchen. But it stimulated Mather's interest in the terraced house as an economical and practical way to build dwellings in a city which still offered everyone a front door and a garden – maximum space for a minimum of materials.

In 1963 when Mather arrived in London looking for work, one of the best firms to work for was generally agreed to be Lyons Israel Ellis. No less a figure than James Stirling had cut his architectural teeth here a decade earlier. Mather went for an interview and was offered a job. At the time, this famous Brutalist practice was designing a series of schools in the West Riding of Yorkshire. The practice split its staff into groups working on individual projects and Mather found himself working with David Wild, who was later to become well known for his own London houses.

The West Yorkshire schools were variants on a theme, built on land prone to mining subsidence. Accordingly, they were designed as single-storey concrete-framed structures, well provided with movement joints, which allowed each function of the school to be expressed separately. They eschewed the use of the then popular CLASP system of school buildings, but there was a style, influenced by Le Corbusier's Maisons Jaoul in Paris: articulated masses, thick timber windows in heavy concrete frames.

After a couple of years working on a school and a teacher-training college for Lyons Israel Ellis, Mather enrolled at the Architectural Association, where Alvin Boyarsky was then teaching. Mather took the urban design course. The school's grand old man of Modernism, Arthur Korn, was a leading light among the tutors. As is often the case with architects who have studied at the AA, Mather continued to have a connection with the school for some time. But after studying Palladio in Vicenza the following summer – his interest was particularly in Palladio's variable grid plan and the siting of his buildings – Mather's first priority was to gain experience in the kind of work that was not being done at that time in the US – large-scale urban residential developments. In London in 1967 most of the interesting jobs were to be found in the public sector. Mather joined a group in the architecture department of the London Borough of Southwark – an inner-city borough south of the River Thames – and began work on the borough's immense slum-replacement programme.

It was about this time that an international competition was announced to design a new town in Finland, 30 kilometres west of Helsinki at a place called Espoo. While Mather was working on type plans during the day, his evenings were spent working up a plan for Espoo with a fellow student from Oregon and the AA's urban design course, Don Genasci. The setting was idyllic; the brief was to create a town of 350,000, complete with all necessary facilities and transport infrastructure.

At first glance, the Mather/Genasci plan for Espoo shows some of the aspects of grid-planning then prevalent in such new towns as Milton Keynes, also conceived around this time. But on closer inspection, it becomes clear that the grid produced by Mather and Genasci is more a linear city that preserved the valley as a park through the centre and threaded its residential streets through the forested hills on either side. It was, notes Mather, his usual way of approaching a project: to take the existing situation and work with that, rather than clear everything away and start from scratch.

At two points the park was bridged by commercial centres, one connected to a subsidiary industrial centre some distance away. The idea was to balance people's destinations so that the rush hour would go in two different directions rather than one. There was an equally simple public transport system based on a double figure-of-eight route which crossed at the centres. It connected all the outlying areas: homes, university, leisure centres. Housing was

In 1967 Mather teamed up with **Don Genasci** to enter the competition for the new **Finnish** town of Espoo, 30km southwest of Helsinki. In their scheme, the valley was preserved as a park running through the town centre. Residential areas were threaded through the surrounding forests

Rick Mather: Urban Approaches

The Mather/Genasci
scheme for Espoo set
up a diagonal grid plan
marching along either
side of the valley,
spanned at its two urban
centres. Their plan for
a linear city won a
generous third prize

High density housing

Medium density housing

Low density housing

Industry

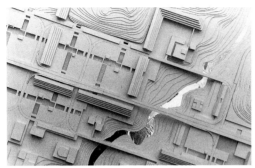

The regular grid of the Espoo Centre model, cut through by the winding river, featured parking and road access on the roof. Buses ran on mezzanines above the glass-roofed streets, leaving the ground completely free for pedestrians

designed to be high-density near the centre (no gardens but handy for shopping and the park), reducing in scale and increasing in separation towards the outskirts (less handy, but with gardens) to produce a variety of house types.

As a worldwide competition, Espoo attracted a high number of completed entries – 350 in all. Outright winner was a scratch team of Polish architects. Mather and Genasci came third, but they weren't aware of it for some time. Nor were the judges at first. Inevitably, the competition was anonymous, with entrants identified only by a reference number. Mather and Genasci had stuck their number on the back of their drawings, where it wasn't immediately discovered. While the announcement party and prize-giving went on in Finland, Mather and Genasci were back in London assuming failure. A month later, somebody thought of unpinning the drawings from the wall, found the numbers and rang London.

Finishing in third place had its upside: there was prize money – quite a lot, until the Finnish mark was devalued by 40 per cent between the time that the winners were announced and the money was paid. Mather's share of the winnings in 1968 was put aside to help buy a house. It came in useful in 1971, when a place came up that was cheap and dilapidated enough for Mather's purposes. Next to a factory in Arlington Road, Camden, it had lain empty since before the Second World War. Later described in glossy magazines as "Regency" (it was in fact William IV), and nothing but a damp shell, a mere 4 metres wide by 6 metres deep, riddled with dry rot, and with a 3-metre-long garden – it was an ideal setting for Mather's desire to experiment with pushing the constraints of the terraced house to their limits.

Once Mather had found a mortgage company prepared to lend on the kind of property more usually associated at the time with speedy demolition, the job was under way. Money was tight; from 1968 Mather supplemented his income with teaching – first, at the Bartlett school at University College London; then at the Polytechnic of Central London; finally, and for five years, at the Architectural Association sharing a unit with Su Rogers and later

Dale Benedict. Teaching had the usual beneficial side-effects for a practising architect: it provided the chance to continue studying, to clarify ideas, and to make contact with good students – some of whom were later to work in Mather's own office.

This was the era of the local-authority improvement grant, which just about balanced the finances on the conversion of Arlington Road. During the day at Southwark, Mather designed housing layouts to be built according to a Danish prefabricated system: duplexes with front doors on to elevated streets. There, he and his colleagues had to deal with a different grants situation, one whereby the Government gave local authorities more cash for building high than for building low. The situation eventually eased, and Southwark was able to allow its architects to try out some low-rise, higher-density schemes, one of which was headed by Mather. In the evenings, he switched attention to the rather different business of putting 145 Arlington Road to rights.

At this time, more private jobs – mainly small house conversions – were coming in from friends and acquaintances. By 1973, with his house completed and attracting attention and income from teaching at the AA and the PCL, there was the prospect of enough steady work for Mather to set up on his own. Rick Mather Architects began in a bedroom at Arlington Road. The firm consisted, apart from the principal, of Pete Roy, one of Mather's students from PCL – and Marj Collins, a retired legal secretary who lived a few doors down the street. The venture was under way.

Chapter two

THE ENGLISHMAN'S HOME

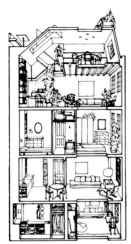

Arlington Road, Mather's own home and first "upside-down house", provided a double-height living space with mezzanine at the top of the house, plus a split-level roof garden

A melodramatic interpretation of Mather's career would present Arlington Road – the first of a series of one-off house projects – as a turning-point. In this account, the house would act as a kind of therapy, an antidote to the large-scale housing projects of Southwark. It could be worked up into something of a road-to-Damascus conversion, a sudden switch from the design of mega-blocks to human-scale restoration. From architect as remote technocratic manipulator, to architect as caring, hands-on craftsman, and so on. Such an account would be singularly misleading.

Mather certainly wanted direct control over what he designed and had built. Arlington Road was a dry run for setting up in private practice, for being in charge rather than being a member of an anonymous group. But there is more of the Southwark-type plan in Arlington Road and subsequent projects than is at first apparent. For one thing, there were actually some very decent dwellings in those unfashionable blocks. The discipline of fitting a fully-functioning architectural entity into a confined and often unforgiving space, of making that space appear to work effortlessly, is something that came to typify Mather's work. He became the transformer of awkward space – a Zen out of a former post office, penthouses out of a sixties office block, a shop out of a crumbling house, sense and sophistication out of the squalid rabbit warren of the AA. More prosaically, he was left with an abiding horror of those twin curses of housing systems: the "cold bridge" and the condensation trap. Mather today can spot a cold bridge from a hundred yards, sense potential trouble spots in an uninsulated external lift tower. He would make a convincing defects trouble-shooter.

The house at 145 Arlington Road presented only virtuous flaws to Mather. To him, the London terraced house was an ideal way to live. Shortly after arriving in England he had absorbed Steen Eiler Rasmussen's *London: The Unique City*. This work from the 1930s, like Muthesius's earlier *Das Englische Haus* gave the view of an onlooker from elsewhere in Europe, championing London's tradition

Arlington Road (below and bottom), a highly successful prototype for Mather, showed how the drawbacks of conventional terraced houses – in particular, dark, compartmented upper floors – could be overcome and transformed through adding light

of terraced housing against the continental model of large urban blocks of flats. For Mather, what counted was Rasmussen's emphasis on the importance of the street and the correspondence between the life of the building and the life of the street.

Arlington Road offered Mather a chance to develop the form of the London terraced house. There was little to spoil, every opportunity to improve. It had a basement, but only a vestigial garden. The view across the street from the ground-floor front room was just that: a view across a shabby street, but it was a workable fragment of the urban grain. Mather started thinking about the merits of living up high in such a house, rather than living downstairs and retiring upwards only to sleep. One of the merits of those big public residential blocks, after all, was the experience of being at high level: something that can be either wonderful or disastrous, depending on the occupants.

So this tall thin house became even taller. The usual basement-and-three-floors arrangement became basement, four internal floors, and then a roof garden. But the top two internal floors acted as one volume, a partly double-height living room with a mezzanine over containing the kitchen and dining area; there was simply not the space to combine kitchen and living areas on one level. Two bedrooms and bathroom were on the floor below, a studio on the ground floor below that. The basement thus became surplus to requirements and could be let out or kept as spare rooms.

The house was an early experiment in the play of light – the upper volumes are flooded with light from the big sloping window to the roof terrace – and the artful disposition of apparently large volumes in what is actually a confined space, aided by mirrors and visually light components such as slender handrails and an open-tread stair. The house also became a showroom for Mather's expanding collection of furniture: some of it, like the Le Corbusier and Rietveld pieces, already acknowledged as classics, others – like Thonet bent wood and Lloyd Loom weave chairs – then little regarded, were picked up in street markets and junk shops. To these, Mather added one of his own early pieces of furniture

Making space: the
high-level sitting-room
at Arlington Road
(opposite) had its
kitchen/dining area
on a mezzanine
above connect to the
roof garden by a
short flight of stairs

design: a rectangular leather sofa à la Corb, but in an exposed
beech frame rather than tubular steel. The piece is also rather
more practical: it converts into a bed simply by pulling out the
bottom frame and dropping the back cushions.

The roof garden was an exercise in creating space out of
nowhere. A tiny area on top at the back of the house provides
enough room for a bench and table; from here steps rise up the
roof slope to the flat roof with railings round. The whole area was
floored with duckboards and covered with plants in containers.

The arrangement of levels in the important upper volumes
is such that there is an interconnection of all the spaces, inside
and outside. It is the opposite of the Victorian norm of the highly
compartmented house, where specific rooms had specific
and isolated functions. Mather likes to cook and likes to talk:
the Arlington Road arrangement allowed him to do both without
dashing in and out of rooms. This house-in-the-sky has some
affinities with the split-level maisonettes that were being designed
in big public housing schemes. Roof garden apart, this is a
universal arrangement, possible three floors up or twenty.
Space was certainly as confined at Arlington Road as it was in
the public sector schemes that Mather was concurrently working
on. But this was a largely secret interior, not disclosing itself to the
street behind the pattern-book façade. Inside, it was an exercise
in extracting a reasonable living space out of a tiny volume.

Such a design must deal with a number of problems that more
conventional house conversions do not: What do you do with water
tanks? Where do you put junk when there is no convenient roof
void? Again, you could argue that the Mather answer was the
public-sector answer: tanks must be contained on a flat roof
(here wooden boxes cloaked with plants) and storage is created
internally. Making a small internal bathroom out of high-ceilinged
early nineteenth-century rooms, Mather lowered the ceiling to
improve the proportion of the bathroom, so forming a space that
could function as an internal attic for bags and cases. But then
Mather is also an organised individual (though he maintains that

this characteristic is more apparent than real). He does not tend to generate clutter.

The Arlington Road house remained Mather's home and office until 1978, with the office expanding and moving down to the lower levels from the bedroom. Then, the upside-down-house principle was transferred more or less intact to Mather's next and current house in Primrose Gardens, Belsize Park. This was another terraced house, but considerably bigger, mid-Victorian rather than William IV, and in a crescent with green space in the middle. Primrose Gardens gave Mather the chance to refine an idea, rather as he was later to refine the Zen idea through numerous metamorphoses. The additional factor here was a respectably-sized back garden at basement level overlooked by a big bay window. By this time, the Mather office was getting bigger: the quality of space and light was far superior to Arlington Road.

Mather repeated the trick. The upside-down house principle had a compelling logic to it: good original rooms can be left largely untouched at lower levels while the poky spaces usually found at the top of such houses could be turned into something better. The upper floors at Primrose Gardens are arranged similarly to Arlington Road, but the size of the house and its existing pitched-roof format gave more space to play around with. There were seven badly proportioned rooms in the area now given over to one big room and a mezzanine. What was merely a large sloping skylight to the roof terrace at Arlington Road here becomes a complete glazed roof section. From the mezzanine you look directly out to the lower level of the roof garden. Other arrangements have changed a little: instead of kitchen-dining on the mezzanine with a sitting-room below, there was enough space to allow the kitchen and dining area to go under the mezzanine, with the sitting room out in the double-height space on the same level. The mezzanine has a bedroom with a small bathroom.

Primrose Gardens was designed to have a working ground floor and a living/entertaining top section. In between is a kind of buffer zone of conventional rooms, including a sitting-room lined with books that acts as a study. The roof garden, big enough to contain a proper garden, is enclosed by high screens of wired glass, preventing views down to the ground-level garden. This is just as well: the tubular steel built-in seating on the lower roof level is cantilevered out over the back of the house. As if on a medieval privy, you are hanging in space. It takes a little while to realise this, if you notice at all; if you do, it takes a little while longer to get used to it.

Improbably, the garden, which includes a barbecue built into the very top of the chimney flue, succeeds in being a private place because it is perched just as high as it is possible to go. From the street it appears far away above the raised mansard storey of the mezzanine area. From its upper level, it is possible to look down even on neighbouring roof extensions. The main living area begins to experiment with the sculptural possibilities of plaster – in contrast to the wooden beams of Arlington Road. There the staircase up was a simple wooden open tread arrangement; here, it is a spiral, enclosed but lightweight, constructed by screwing and gluing plywood stringers, treads and risers, and stiffening the whole with a reinforced outer shell of plaster.

There is virtually no evidence of the original house at this level: where the Victorian hardwood balustrade terminates from the rooms below is a point of division. A deliberately Heath Robinson pulley-and-counterweight system seals off the top of the stairs from below with doors moving both horizontally and vertically.

Mather arranged the garden down below as a sequence of outdoor "rooms" – effectively three zones of vegetation, ranging from a kitchen garden nearest the house to a tended wilderness at the back, populated with plants from Oregon. Half-way down, the flank walls are breached to give cross-views into neighbouring gardens. The garden was used more when Mather's studio, with all its staff, occupied the ground and basement floors. Once the studio moved to a far bigger space in Camden Town, its old quarters became guest rooms: Mather now sees this garden mostly from above.

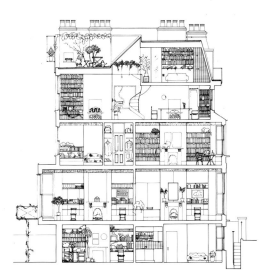

Upside-down house Mark 2: Mather's house and office at Primrose Gardens followed the pattern of his earlier house, but on a grander scale. A roof garden seat was cantilevered off the back of the house

Light is everything in the upper reaches of Primrose Gardens. Full-width glazing to the roof terrace (right and below) is at eye level from the bedroom mezzanine. The minimal stair in plywood and plaster shell (opposite) rises from the living/ kitchen area to a mezzanine bedroom and the roof

Rick Mather: Urban Approaches

Between the two Mather houses came a rather more radical exercise in living over the shop, and the first project that gained Mather's fledgling practice serious attention. Peter Eaton is an antiquarian bookseller who had started out selling from a barrow on the Portobello Road. Success allowed him to expand into an early nineteenth-century terrace house-turned-shop. Eaton, his business still growing, needed more shelf space. He asked the practice of Colquhoun and Miller for advice, as they had recently completed the then largest architectural bookshop in the world, Weinreb. Unable to take on the commission themselves, Mather found himself recommended for the job, so he went to Holland Park to look at the shop. It was, he discovered, a wonder that the place was still standing. Creeping decay had overtaken the areas away from public view. Urgent restructuring was needed. Mather also discovered that Eaton needed a vast increase in his selling and storage space. The completely rebuilt shop was the first of Mather's transparent-fronted, half-public, half-private commercial spaces that were later to be refined into the Zen restaurant concept.

The ground floor was removed altogether and the whole site was excavated to basement level. With the help of John Vincent, the structural engineer then teaching with Mather at the AA, the top two floors were supported on a steel frame, effectively becoming a separate building – like Chareau's Maison de Verre. The new bookshop took shape in the void left beneath. At the end of the process, the Eatons found themselves with a bookshop arranged on seven levels, so that every inch of wall space was accessible to the public and visible from a single cashier's position. Because the shop extends to either side of the plan of the old house, daylight could be brought in right down to the service and selling areas in the basement through roof-lights and a glazed section of floor.

Many of Mather's later concerns are to be found in the Peter Eaton shop: most notably, the dissolution of divisions between the interior and the street. A glass skin on the street line slopes back

Peter Eaton's bookshop was the first job for Mather's own practice, and the first of his interiors to open up fully to the street

a metre at the top to connect with the solid elements of the shop front. However, Eaton's budget was necessarily low and the contractor far from sophisticated – butt-jointing the large panes of glass would have been asking for trouble. Mather had instead to frame the glass in metal, a method he was to employ at his first Zen restaurant. But it worked: the skin, transparent or reflecting, depending on the relative light levels inside and outside the shop, does dissolve inside into outside. To Eaton's slight surprise, he felt that he was back selling on the street again. Mather could notch up a curious first: he had designed the first purpose-built antiquarian bookshop in London for 50 years.

William Gillespie and his wife, psychiatrists, were also in a way looking for a shop. Approaching Mather shortly after the completion of his Primrose Gardens house, they wanted a house which could include consulting rooms and, they said, they wanted it to be just like Mather's own place (there are advantages to having your office in your own house). When Mather found a suitable property for conversion for his new clients, they expressed doubts: this was no tall narrow terraced house, but rather a wider 1840s semi-detached villa in Chalk Farm. Approached through the garden, with stairs entrance and service rooms placed in a side bay to the main house, it had more of a suburban than urban feel. A sketch design and models convinced them to go ahead, remodelling the top two floors to make one large volume, with the mezzanine over, provided the scope for a more sculptural interior. The right angles appropriate to a narrow terraced house here begin to be subverted to curves. The simple device of leaving the fireplace aperture of the former upper floor hanging in space imparts a surreal quality.

The Mather roof terrace (descended, surely, from the decks of the Oregon timber houses) again makes its appearance, set in the side of the main pitched roof and accessible from the mezzanine. Light is brought into the main space from above. The edge to the stair stands proud – a device used over a decade later in the Now and Zen restaurant.

From the start of the 1980s, Mather's practice began to attract rather bigger commissions than such one-off domestic conversions. However, that early experience remained important: his familiarity with the pattern of the London terraced house stood him in good stead when it came to the Architectural Association refurbishment, which began in 1978 and lasted five years. Residential work also continued to appear among the bigger projects, some built, some not.

Among the unbuilt was a scheme that was Mather's first departure from the city context since he left Oregon at the start of the 1960s. A once substantial country house in Lincolnshire had been reduced by time and various uncaring owners to a ruinous base, still retaining a grand approach, a monumental gateway and a corner tower. The brief from the clients – a local farmer and his wife – was somehow to make a much smaller, single-storey dwelling out of this unpromising material. Mather attempted to do so by the apparently paradoxical means of designing a second tower to counterbalance the first, diagonally across a courtyard. He resolved this apparent defiance of the brief by putting all the guest rooms in the tower. Rooms for his clients were then arranged in a single-storey row, facing south, to create one side of the courtyard. In order to give this block the scale its situation demanded, Mather designed, not the usual low pitched roof, but a high wall with a valley roof behind. Another side of the courtyard – not needed for accommodation – was given mass by being converted into a walled garden, linking the new house with the existing tower. The third side was defined by great wedges of hedging, and the fourth – including the grand entrance arch – was completed with a high conventional hedge.

By this means, the brief for one smallish country dwelling was refined into the remaking of a substantial architectural complex as economically as possible. The scheme did not proceed, but it was important as a test bed for future projects. Apart from anything else, it was Mather's first attempt at re-inventing the valley roof (or "butterfly roof" when it oversails the walls). Encountered

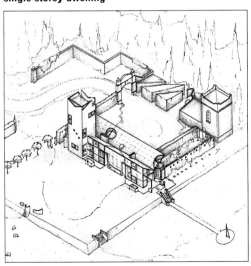

Creating context in the country – this Lincolnshire project knitted existing fragments of a house into a courtyard complex complete with a second tower. The brief had been for a modest single-storey dwelling

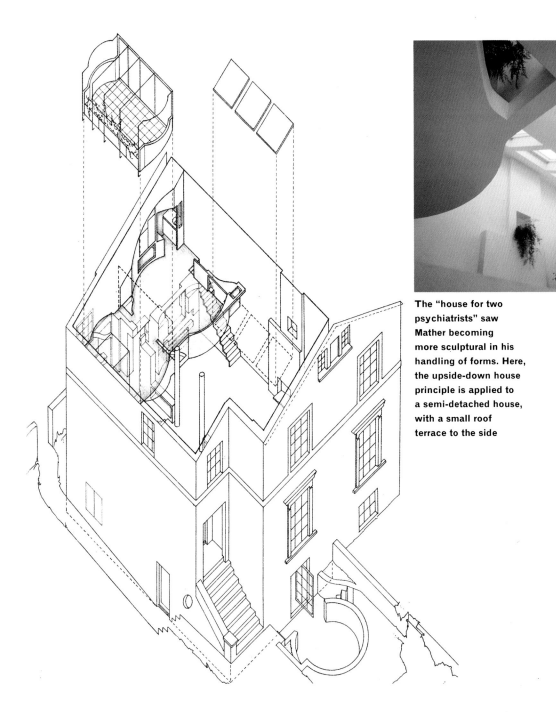

The "house for two psychiatrists" saw Mather becoming more sculptural in his handling of forms. Here, the upside-down house principle is applied to a semi-detached house, with a small roof terrace to the side

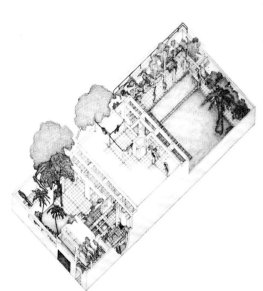

**The Latif residential
compound in Khartoum,
Sudan, 1982 – two
houses in a formal,
shady water garden**

so often in the London houses he dealt with, starting with his own at Arlington Road, the valley roof in the eighteenth and nineteenth centuries was a cheap way of concealing the roof pitch, the valley usually running back at right angles to the house front behind a parapet. For the Lincolnshire project, Mather swung the valley through 90 degrees to run along the spine of the building, allowing high walls front and back, and the possibility of projecting eaves that lead the eye even higher. The run-off from a valley roof demands careful detailing simply because rainwater is taken to the centre and away rather than being thrown off at the edges. But it offers concealment for roof-lights, plant and suchlike. As usual with Mather, the butterfly roof idea was refined through successive projects until it became a virtual trademark, most noticeably in the heroic tilted hat of the Pennington Street office building in 1991.

Residential work, slotted among other jobs in the years to come, varied from the model of the upside-down house. The year 1982 saw a design for a residential compound in Khartoum, Sudan: two big houses, a pool and water garden. Later came a scheme for Charles and Doris Saatchi in London's St John's Wood: the proposal was to renovate a nineteenth-century Hansel-and-Gretel Gothic fantasy so that it would be more habitable and could house some of the Saatchis' art collection. The Saatchis, however, chose to move to Mayfair instead.

It was in 1986 that Mather dipped his toe into London's Docklands with a small development based around a renovated school building in Bermondsey. Mather, though, had to come to terms with the commercial sector: not least, the coarsening of detailing that many developer-led projects involve. These collaborations were not always ideal from his point of view, but they demonstrated a confidence in handling urban projects on a steadily increasing scale.

One commission, in 1988, came from the London Docklands Development Corporation itself: a study for a new Light Railway station at South Quay. Mather expanded the brief into a strategy for urbanising the Isle of Dogs by showing how the negative space

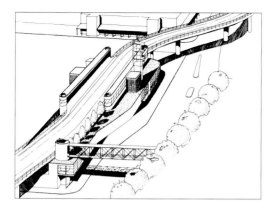

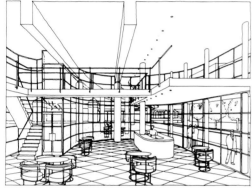

An interest in pre-war
Modernism surfaces in
Mather's study for a
light railway station at
South Quay in London's
Docklands (top).
A café/retail complex
under the elevated tracks
(above) suggests how
this wasted space
could have been used
to create a "street"

under the elevated track either side of the station could be used for shops and cafés to make a proper city street. The LDDC liked the proposal. It's implementation awaits an upturn in the economy and the property market. The largest piece of urban planning since the Espoo competition in 1967, however, came when Mather was asked to help plan a vast scheme of 10,000 homes, offices, shops, light industry, a marina and park elsewhere in Docklands. The scheme, still classified secret by its developers, fell by the wayside.

Other projects from the period provided the control over design and detailing that he prefers. Art dealer Margaret Lipworth took Mather on to rebuild her part of Wychcombe Studios, a development of Victorian artists' studios with north-lit spaces typical of the period. Lipworth's unit had been badly cut about over the years, but here for once Mather had a shell that had been originally a double-height space flooded with light. Stripped back to its simple volume as the living space, it was perfect with a kitchen (tucked under the U-shaped upper gallery) holding its usual Mather-like conversation with the living space. More complex were the spaces in the existing rear extension. Here, where the bedrooms and bathrooms were placed, light is brought down from above via a pyramidal conservatory roof. A translucent bridge crosses the space: access, via a spiral plaster shell stair à la Primrose Gardens, is through a cylindrical apse connecting the front and rear volumes. By opening up sliding doors in the apse, south light is brought into the usually north-lit living space. So it functions as either a gallery or a home, with natural light from north or south, according to mood.

To go from Arlington Road in 1972 to the house in Chester Row that Mather completed nearly 20 years later for Professor and Mrs Dworkin is to see an obsession worked out almost to the ultimate degree. Only an extra third of a metre in width distinguishes the plan of the spec house in shabby Camden from the spec house in up-market Belgravia, both built in the 1830s, so unvarying was the pattern of terraced house building in London. Mather's response over the years has followed its own pattern, a pattern almost of

Wychcombe Studios (opposite, below and bottom), built in the 1870s for artists, were originally designed to maximise north light. Mather stripped the space of later additions and created one simple volume, brought light into the back via a glass pyramid roof, and joined front and rear with a cylindrical apse

reversal. It is a curious mix of respect for the ground-plan and radical disagreement with the type-plan, with the hierarchy of spaces contained within it. "The curse of most London terraced houses," Mather remarks, "is that they are just a collection of cupboards off a staircase."

Chester Row, like most of Mather's houses, was in a dangerously bad state when he first encountered it in 1987, but was nonetheless officially listed as being of historic importance. Even to design something that peeped over the top of the façade was forbidden. In any event, Mather's spatial responses were changing. The challenge here was still to make bigger rooms, but not by creating a separate upper kingdom. Instead, the house is opened up vertically towards the rear, preserving the plan while slicing surgically through the section. Mather describes it as a "considered play on interconnected volumes". Spaces have ceased to be merely, or even mostly, functional. No one could pretend that a house actively needs a double-height glazed conservatory at the rear that reveals the transformed inner workings of the house as if it were a back-to-front doll's house, or as if the garden were a street, and the house were a Zen restaurant talking to it. This is a private conversation: the listed frontage is still there, unchanged.

This project took a long time to complete, not least because it displays design standards usually missing from domestic interiors: a free-standing kitchen in the manner of a highly-lacquered Chinese puzzle box: a built-in hi-fi cabinet with its free-sailing glass top like a refined restaurant bar; materials in the details such as American ash, waxed white plaster, steel that is oiled or lacquered, polished slate and acid-washed white Portland stone. The domestic interior as an inhabited sculptural space – something that began to emerge coherently in Mather's work with the Gillespie house of the late 1970s – here reaches an advanced state. It is serious stuff. But a certain dry wit informs Mather's functionalist description of the big plane trees in the garden: not trees as such, rather an automatically opening filter to protect the glazed rear elevation from the summer sun.

Chapter three

INTO
THE LIONS'
DEN

At the AA, Mather's most radical work was in the basement. Party walls were removed to allow the long restaurant space across two house widths (top). Closing the axis is the Triangle bookshop (above)

No gigantic perceptual leap is needed to move from the design of a small, complex interior to that of an entire built area. A city can be seen as a collection of rooms and passageways; a house can be viewed as a metropolis. What can be argued, nonetheless, is that the specific should proceed to the general: better perhaps that a designer of discrete urban elements should become a master-planner than vice-versa.

In Mather's case, the shift from discrete designer to master-planner occurred almost imperceptibly. When invited by the council of the Architectural Association in 1978 to embark on a substantial renovation of the AA, the task was on one level the creation of an educational masterplan: to impose some order on to a compact complex that had developed willy-nilly over the years and had ceased to make sense (if it ever had) in planning terms. On another level, here were three Georgian terraced houses in a rough state in a splendid, historically important, city square. Who better than Mather, with his experience of the London terrace, to put them to rights?

This was, intentionally or not, a test for Mather. For him to take on the Architectural Association was to enter the lions' den. As the premier school of architecture in the United Kingdom, if not the world, there was an awful weight of history and nostalgia for the Oregonian architect to contend with. He was dealing with the collective past of the British architectural Establishment, with Alvin Boyarsky, a figure that the said establishment was to regard with mingled awe and unease right up to his death in 1990. A high-risk commission then – one that prefigured his later work at the University of East Anglia, where he had to get along with the hovering spirits of Sir Denys Lasdun and Sir Norman Foster.

The AA work proceeded in phases through to 1984, and so overlapped with the start of the East Anglia project, coincided with domestic jobs, and was completed just before the commission for the first Zen. Many concerns came together here.

The Bedford Square houses dated from the 1780s, part of the composition of builder Thomas Leverton in which each side of

Mather's scheme for
the AA library set out to
make all books in the
collection accessible,
with upper-level
walkways in the two
main rear rooms to
maximise wall space.
A glass turret acted as
a reading/lookout area
over the courtyard

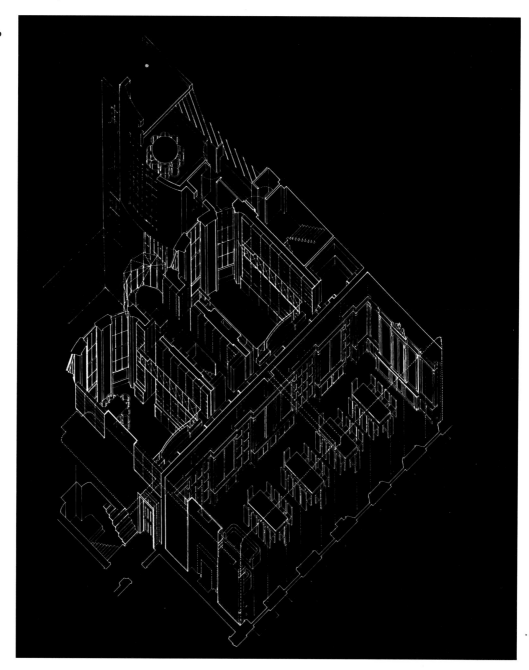

Into the Lions' Den

The AA slide library, previously a shop, was filled out with filing draws, hanging plants and reference tables

the square, composed of grand three-storey houses, is unified beneath a central pediment to read as a separate palace. Three of the houses on the western side, numbers 34 to 36, had been combined to form the Architectural Association, school and club, in the 1920s. The subsequent growth of the school led to the planning mess that Mather had to deal with. In addition, Bedford Square was jerry-built. For all its pre-eminence as one of London's last two remaining intact Georgian squares (the other being the courtyard defined by the ranges of Sir William Chambers' Somerset House), it was something of a miracle that great chunks of the square had not simply fallen down over the years. Mather was used to suspect terraced houses, but the three which formed the AA were quite remarkably shoddy behind the façades. One end of a party wall had dropped 15cm, and was reportedly built on the silt bed of a former pond. Some of the foundations, to judge by the neat 30.5cm × 5.1cm hole running through them (now filled), had been built off flat builders' planks that had rotted away over the next two hundred years.

It was, however, the organisational aspects of the AA that mainly concerned Mather. There was no direct route from the main front door to the studio block at the rear. If you were unfamiliar with the place, it was near-impossible to find the basement lecture theatre. One of the grand ground-floor rooms was compromised by having to accommodate the college reception and office. There was an almost liturgical need for the premises to reflect better the activities planned by Boyarsky, not least his desire to make the AA a centre for public exhibitions and talks. The AA, therefore, had to become a more publicly accessible building. So Mather drew up his first masterplan for an educational establishment.

Making the circulation routes simpler and more comprehensible was the first step. The key was to cut a new direct route from front to back, and to place a new reception area directly on this route. That freed the grand room fronting on to Bedford Square, which was combined with the room behind to form an exhibitions gallery. The room was discreetly air-conditioned from a unit concealed

The big ground-floor gallery space has such well concealed dividing doors that they are never used. Plant holders are part of a range of furniture that Mather designed for the job

above the central bay. The brief was to make the gallery divisible. Borrowing basic features common to terraced-houses, Mather provided big concealed folding doors to separate the two rooms when necessary. They are perhaps too well concealed, and in fact have only been used once; the room is now perceived as a single space.

Similarly, the lecture hall to the right of the entrance lobby was made to work better as a volume. Mather later observed that, when complete, his intention had been to make it look as if nothing had happened to it at all. The lighting, a combination of new downlighters flush with the ceiling and existing 1930s bracket chrome-bowl uplighters, newly restored, were the giveaway and for acoustic reasons it was carpeted rather than hard-floored.

In the basement, more radical restructuring was possible. As in his other conversions, the best rooms of the houses, on the ground floor, were preserved, but this time a big new volume was opened up below them. The three-house width of the AA premises allowed for horizontal reorganisation rather than exploitation of the vertical section that preoccupied Mather in his domestic work. The basement was a warren of little rooms, much altered in the past, with only the front windows original. Mather restored the windows and behind them carved out a vista running the combined width of the three houses. The Triangle Bookshop and an access passage occupied one house width, and a restaurant ran across the width of the other two houses. All of this involved combining several rooms and partially removing one of those suspect party walls, which had the benefit of strengthening the building's shaky foundations.

The white-tiled servery, kitchen, and private dining room (linked to the courtyard) were in the bays to the rear, so the view through was uninterrupted. Finished in white, with terracotta quarry-tile flooring, glass-topped tables and blue canvas chairs, the long restaurant space was defined by globe pendant lights, and its end wall mirrored to double its apparent length. What had been the old school supplies shop in the rear of the basement became the new

The original period detail was carefully restored and modern light AC and AV equipment concealed in the lecture theatre (above). As in the basement, an axis across all three houses was opened through the middle. The AA bar (opposite) with furniture by Mather has a touch of the nightclub

slide library. It was day-lit from above and expanded by curving round it the passage through to the back stairs. The slide library was fitted out with three big reference tables, lined with light wood filing drawers to waist level, hung with plants, and adorned with blow-ups of Frank Yerbury's photos of 1930s American skyscrapers.

Later, when the AA work was finished, Mather was asked to find ways to improve Richard Branson's subterranean nightclub Heaven underneath London's Charing Cross station. The success of the club – it is a legendary and long-lived venue – had brought problems of congestion. "We helped them sort out some of the problems," was Mather's only comment later. This project, again, involved producing a masterplan as well as designing a new quiet bar; there was only limited supervision, and it was further exposure to the particular problems of bars and restaurants. The AA had already provided Mather with his first opportunity to do a bar as well as the furniture that went in it, and was to prove a rehearsal for the later Zen restaurants.

Student bars conventionally relish squalor: Mather intended this to be conspicuously different. The marble-topped AA bar was stationed against the wall opposite the fireplace in a standard Georgian room. As with so many London theatre bars where space is similarly restricted, the wall behind was mirrored to give the illusion of double the volume. This had the effect of turning the rectangular bar into a free-standing square. The corners were contrived as mirrored returns and so appear to dissolve. A variation of this device is to be found in the stout Victorian gateposts leading to Mather's front door in Primrose Gardens. There, an angled slot of mirror glass in each post at eye level creates the fleeting illusion that the heavy capstones are floating in free space. Appearing to defy, or at any rate to cock a snook at, the force of gravity was to become another Mather hallmark.

The AA bar featured what has become a characteristic of Mather's bars, the area around was floored in stone – the countertop appears to float above its base. Around it are the first of the bar stools that were to become a family of furniture for Zen:

simple chromed steel legs with circular black leather seats, base and foot-rest, paying homage to Eileen Gray. Mather varied the design for tables and for plant stands throughout the AA.

What makes the bar more than just the usual peak-hours-only space is the fact that it lies athwart one of Mather's circulation routes running to the studios at the back. A similar tactic was employed in the roof terrace, a half-landing above the bar, where as an outdoor extension to the bar, it's fine in fine weather, but is also another way of getting to the studios. The spaces have a dual function: places to move through and places to pause in.

Mather's masterplan for the AA was never quite completed, however. A final phase was to have made the school's library easier to use on the Peter Eaton principle of covering every available inch of wall space with bookshelves, accessed from a narrow gallery in the two big rear rooms. Bringing in daylight as always, Mather planned a glass turret of a conservatory overlooking the courtyard between the two rear rooms. However, the main reading room fronting Bedford Square on the lofty first floor level, the august heart of the library, was to remain intact.

The library scheme would have had the benefit of making all books in the AA's collection instantly accessible and allowed for some future expansion. At that time, only a third of the collection was available – the majority of the books was stored elsewhere, to be distributed only on special order. Nevertheless, the new scheme was never put into effect because the Architectural Association then entered yet another phase of financial and political crisis. Mather was not surprised to find that this was a normal feature of an extended commission. Early in the process, in 1979, Boyarsky had faced students hostile to what was seen by some as an extravagant, image-led remodelling, done more for the benefit of visiting dignitaries than for the students themselves. Such feelings had died down by the end of the work.

Despite the fact that the *Architect's Journal*, then very much an establishment magazine, described the upstairs bar as "flashy", the journal admitted that the bar sat quite happily in the Georgian room. The more internationally-minded *Architectural Review*, meanwhile, declared that Mather's style was cool and label-less. "Any other interior treatment would probably date too easily," it declared. In sum, Mather had emerged unscathed from the lions' den.

By this time, though, Mather had landed the commission for his biggest job to date. The University of East Anglia at Norwich had, like many of Britain's new universities, become an architectural showground for some of the big names of the day. Planned in the early 1960s by Sir Denys Lasdun and part-completed to his ziggurat designs by 1970, the campus had subsequently been through various hands. Bernard Feilden inherited the mantle of masterplanner and modified Lasdun's original concept of buildings forming architectural hills and valleys in the landscape. But it was Norman Foster, with his Sainsbury Centre for the Visual Arts in 1978, who created a new focus at the western end of the UEA campus.

UEA always intended to expand, and the Sainsbury Centre was in a way a side-issue. The man with responsibility for the expansion was Gordon Marshall, the estates' officer for the university who had been Foster's main point of contact at UEA. On Foster's recommendation, the university invited Mather to consider how best to place new facilities on the relatively undeveloped north side of Lasdun's "Teaching Wall". The Teaching Wall is a megastructure, marked at one end by the entrance to the whole campus, and at the other, at an angle relating to the alignment of Lasdun's original expansion plan, by the Sainsbury Centre. Up to this point all major development at the university had been on the other side of the wall, focusing on the campus lake known as "the Broad". Mather's initial brief for the UEA was to place a small building for the School of Information Systems or SYS on this northern flank. True to form, Mather set about creating a sense of place to locate the building. He defined three elements: first, a new building acting as a wall to intercept movement along the north side of Lasdun's behemoth; second, a gateway in that

The new **EDU, SYS** and **CRU** buildings to the north of the "Teaching Wall" and the Sainsbury Centre were the first stage in a development plan for this western sector of the campus which was to be extended later by the residential "snake"

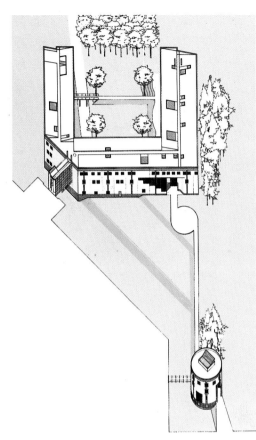

The above drawing, for Mather's first stand-alone new building, at the University of East Anglia shows the relationship of the courtyard building and cylinder next to the "Teaching Wall". Both the CRU building (opposite) and the EDU building are used to define routes

wall to announce a presence and define a route through; and finally, a garden defining the new spaces as a reward for following the visual signals correctly, and a recompense for not having a view of the Broad on the other side of the complex.

As with the aborted project for the house in Lincolnshire, this was an exercise in making much out of relatively little. Fortuitously, UEA's needs quickly expanded: the university also needed new premises for the School of Education (EDU) and for the Climatic Research Unit (CRU). All together this was, at 4650 square metres, three times the area originally asked for. Mather could put flesh on the bones of the original scheme, but it was still a challenge to confront the flank of the Teaching Wall alongside.

The valley roof principle, as employed on the Lincolnshire house project, was summoned to assist. The bigger departments – SYS and the EDU – were placed in one big building around three sides of a courtyard garden. The Climatic Research Unit was originally part of this building, but late in the day, when the designs were ready to go out to tender, SYS found that they needed more space. To release the space, Mather placed the CRU in a separate, gatehouse building.

The valley roof of the main building served to provide the maximum height for the walls of the big courtyard building, and its apparent height was increased with a vertical treatment to the façades. The glazed blockwork was laid vertically and shaded to define base, middle and top; punched windows were arranged into narrow bays, two at a time, marked by vertical divisions; every second bay was further divided by narrow vertical slit windows running the full height of the façade.

Many of these proportioning tricks are employed on traditional terraced houses. The effect was to allow the new building to visually stand up to its Lasdun "big brother" alongside. Mather then housed the CRU in a separate cylinder at a sufficient distance from the main new block to act as a gatehouse to the new dispensation of landscape, conceived as outdoor rooms, and buildings beyond. The cylinder, visible from the main campus

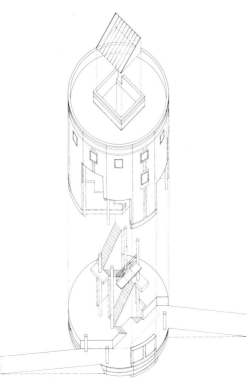

The **CRU** building (above) is a node on Mather's circulation route and a gatehouse to the **EDU** building (opposite). Much of the money went on interiors, where the sparing use of decorative masonry led some to detect Postmodern tendencies

entrance, tells the visitor that there is this complex beyond. As with the bar at the AA, both buildings are used to define routes. To walk along the north side of the Teaching Wall from the campus entrance to the Sainsbury Centre takes you first through the cylindrical gatehouse, then through the main entrance of the courtyard block, out the other side across the open end of the courtyard, and to a junction of the path that leads you to the ground-level entrances of the Sainsbury Centre. Both of the Mather buildings are linked to the Teaching Wall, rather than being free-standing objects. Both stand close to the mother building and are physically plugged into it, their geometries relating to it.

The model that Mather wanted most of all to avoid for his two new buildings was the academic rooms-off-a-corridor approach, something he dislikes as much as the cupboards-off-a-stair format of many terraced houses. With a tight budget and a complicated brief, it was a difficult task to design generous spaces, but by being efficient about the arrangement of rooms, it proved to be possible. The circulation space in the big building is interrupted at frequent intervals by vertical spaces running through all three storeys and bringing in natural light. Spaces such as the three-storey entrance to EDU were not in the brief (nor was the courtyard outside), but they have turned out to be useful for the kind of ancillary activities that all university departments generate: exhibitions, concerts, meetings. Classes as well as parties take place in the courtyard, a bonus that the University Grants Committee which used to set the cost yardsticks for such schemes had not anticipated their budgets could extend to.

For the first time in his career, these two buildings raised the issue of Mather's architectural style. Completed in 1984 and 1985, they were the first entirely new-built schemes that he had done since setting up in practice more than a decade before. For some, used to the Modernist clarity of Mather's interiors, these showed Postmodern tendencies. They are certainly as Po-mo as Mather ever got, which means not very. But the façades do employ certain devices that could be taken that way: for instance, the stepped

Mather's interventions
at **UEA** as masterplanner
and architect aim to tie
together the straggling
campus. Cranked blocks
of student residences
(3 and 4) make urban
spaces, as do his earlier
EDU/SYS and **CRU**
buildings (1 and 2).
Work began on the new
Drama Centre (5) in 1991

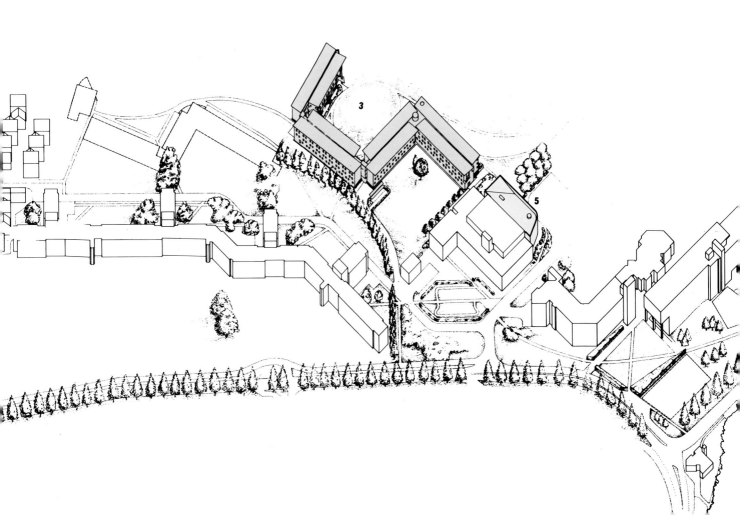

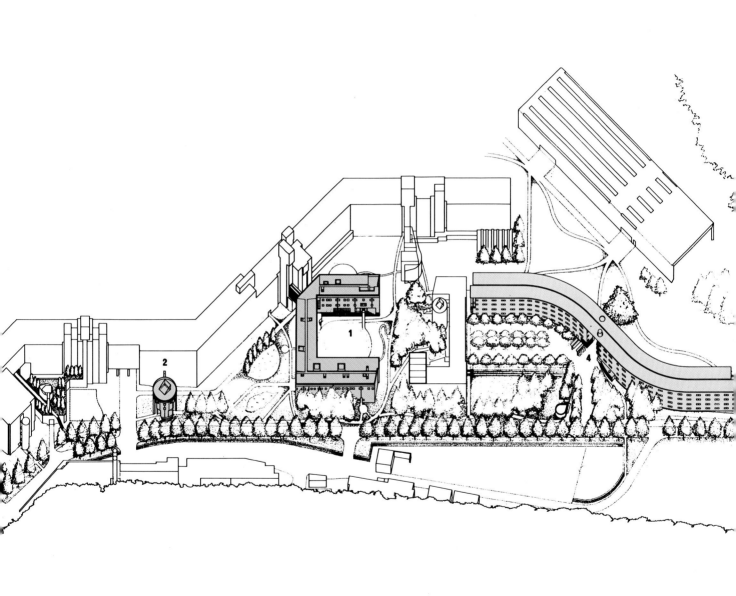

glazing that breaks into the masonry to the left of the main entrance; the modest patterning of the masonry itself; the semi-formal landscaping; the whole idea of the punched wall rather than the sleek skin, epitomised by the Sainsbury Centre, then still in its original aluminium carapace.

Mather found himself facing such questions of style when he presented the partly-completed scheme in a lecture at the Royal Institute of British Architects in February 1984 – the packed hall indicating that he had by this time achieved something approaching cult status. Boyarsky, who introduced the lecture, offered his view that Mather was employing classical elements precisely because Modernism had never found a satisfactory way to treat elevations. Mather conceded that Boyarsky was "half right", while at the same time remarking that he himself had been schooled in Modernism, a set of values that clings to you throughout life as much as, for instance, Catholicism. Whether the comments stung or not, it is hard to say. Certainly he has used rather different elements, more to do with the spirit of pre-war Modernism, to compose the façades of his later big buildings.

The progression from this modest beginning to Mather's appointment in 1988 as consultant masterplanner for UEA was a logical, almost inevitable transition. In developing the north wall buildings, Mather and the UEA had to consider the long-term development of this part of the campus. Both agreed that nothing should be done which would hinder future development. At the same time Mather pressed for some kind of overall strategy for the campus, ground rules for future development.

From the start Mather understood his task quite clearly: to re-urbanise the spreading campus. UEA can be a most dispiriting place on a wet blowy day, and is not readily comprehensible as a place to wander around. On the plus side (particularly on a fine day), it does achieve something of that original vision of an optimistic, futuristic centre of learning set in an ideal landscape. The problem Mather perceived was that the campus was incomplete – not only in its overall plan and diversity of uses but

Bringing light into the EDU building, and creating big high-circulation spaces, proved possible on the kind of budget normally reserved for dumb boxes with cubicles off dark corridors

Snaking between the
works of Lasdun and
Foster, the western range
of low-energy student
residences at **UEA**
establish a balance
between the old and new
parts of campus. Shared
houses form the lower
floors; flats on the top
layer have separate
access. The butterfly
roof results in interesting
geometry at the block's
chamfered western end

also, crucially, in the connections. Like the Aztec pyramids that its original residential buildings deliberately echo, it implied the existence of a greater, more homogeneous civilisation.

This is always the way with Mather – he would find an excuse for an urban framework, one suspects, in the middle of the Sahara – but at UEA it makes perfect sense. Virtually a town in its own isolation, the fabric of the campus was incomplete in the same way that a cleared site renders an inner city landscape incomplete. In this case, the fact that the campus has never been fully completed in no way lessens the validity of comparison with a spoilt inner city. This is a place to knit together. Fortunately, the university was continuing to plan for expansion through the next 25 years, so providing Mather with opportunities to place new buildings strategically to make the connections.

The most pressing need was for student residences. UEA is right on the edge of Norwich, in a sylvan landscape but quite a distance from the bedsits where many students live. At the same time, the city has an acute shortage of rented homes for its non-student population. Lasdun's original masterplan allowed for more housing ziggurats on campus, but the time, the inclination and the money for that kind of architecture had passed.

Mather developed an approach to housing that could apply to most configurations that the site would demand: a spine of accommodation that could define courtyards, form walls, and follow circulation routes. This was his opportunity to contribute to the development of the English terraced house, and in a sense the spines of accommodation that he has developed for UEA are logical extensions of the idea of the one-off upside-down house: one type of dwelling beneath, and another type up above. However, here the two varieties of accommodation are separated and put into different tenancies. The housing is on four floors: the three lower floors are houses shared by ten students, each with its own front door on to the street. Above is a layer of flats for two students apiece, with access from the ends of each range of houses.

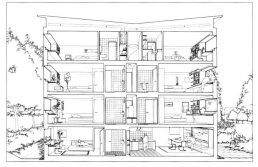

The first block of residences to be built on this model is at the eastern end of the campus: a cranked sequence of four blocks linked roughly at right angles to each other to define, with the aid of tree planting and landscaping, two big "outdoor rooms". The buildings and the landscape fill in what was previously one of UEA's big gaps, a hard-surfaced games area that effectively isolated the eastern ranges of the campus from the centre. The new housing forms a link here, replacing a path that staff and students used as a short-cut across the campus with a pedestrian street. A further planned phase of similarly cranked blocks beyond will finally tie in the easternmost extremities of the campus.

More controversial for a time was Mather's second range of new housing, designed as part of his planned continuation of the development on the western side of the campus, north of and emerging from the shadow of the Teaching Wall. This had to negotiate two tricky hurdles: some woodland previously deemed sacrosanct, and the possibly even more sacrosanct proximity of the Sainsbury Centre, that has achieved something approaching "ancient monument" status.

Mather's proposal was for a double-curved row of terraced residences, opened in the middle by a "gateway" defined by an access tower and a roof that sails right over the gap. The terrace navigates a course between the Scylla of the Sainsbury Centre and the ghostly Charybdis of Lasdun's original (unbuilt) expansion plan. At its eastern end, it aligns with the south wing of Mather's mid-eighties block, allowing space for three more additions to the teaching faculties that will, when built, complete a sequence of buildings and spaces running right across the north edge of the campus. The break between the two long curved blocks aligns with the north-western end of the Sainsbury Centre. There is even a relationship, in form if not in geometry, with the Crescent Wing extension to the Sainsbury Centre, also designed by Foster, that opened to the south-east of the original shed in 1991.

The scheme got approval, which along with the other project meant that Mather found himself with 800 residences to build – the

The range of residences breaks at the centre of its S-curve, allowing views through to the Sainsbury Centre and giving stairway and lift access to the upper-level flats

biggest commission he had yet undertaken. A drama centre was later added, all three projects to be completed by autumn 1993. All this was in the public sector, approved at a time of deep economic recession in the UK. The standard of fit-out is higher than most student accommodation – ensuite showers, better kitchens, living and dining areas than usual – on the principle that this makes the residences more attractive to the lucrative vacation conference trade which universities need to subsidise their students the rest of the year.

The housing, with its oversailing butterfly roof, is important not only for the contribution it makes to an important urban form, but also for its low-energy qualities. Mather has never seen the energy aspects of his buildings as their prime generator (with the interesting exception of a self-build house he designed for his sister and her family in northern Alberta in 1981). He takes it as conventional wisdom that just happens not to be observed everywhere. So the UEA houses are deep-plan, super-insulated and with heat recovery systems, meaning that no central heating is needed. Designed also with low-maintenance finishes, the homes should remove one of the main fears of public-sector development officers: continuing and increasing running costs.

The curved terrace ends in a complex terminal geometry of curving wall and split butterfly roof, the end chamfered and divided to form a final stack of balconies looking west, away from the university. Rather than a city wall, this is another kind of gatehouse, forming an apex and an introduction to the sequence of spaces beyond.

Chapter four

THE RESTAURANT AS URBAN THEATRE

ZENW3 in Hampstead (opposite) marked a departure for restaurant design, as Lawrence Leung commissioned Mather for the first in a series of theatrical and sophisticated eating spaces. The principles of all later Zens are enshrined herein: the use of glass and light, an upper mezzanine level, painstaking attention to detail, and not a bad seat in the house

It is worth taking a look into the kitchen of Now and Zen in London's St Martin's Lane, Mather's most recent exercise in his global chain of Zens for restaurateur Lawrence Leung. All restaurant kitchens are hot sweaty places, and none more so than your average Chinese, where fast high-temperature cooking in a wok is essential. In Now and Zen, you are faced with a row of quite fearsome gas burners, each one looking like an exhaust nozzle of a Saturn V moon rocket. "These," Mather remarks, "could heat a whole side of a street."

Now consider several of these devices roaring away on a busy evening in a kitchen just off the downstairs eating area. Mather had to dispose of all this heat without it affecting the environment of the restaurant, which itself has to be extensively cooled just to remove the heat of people gathered for conversation and food. A steady breeze blows through the kitchen as a result: 60 air changes per hour. This tells you two things. One is that that there is more to designing a Zen than playing about with glass. The other is that the total effect of a Zen – what you see as a customer – is created out of a budget that has to include a sobering provision for hidden services. Reflect also that Mather is a low-energy enthusiast, engaged at the time of Now and Zen in designing student residences at the University of East Anglia that will use virtually no energy at all. It is a relief to find that at least some of the immense amount of heat generated by those burners is reclaimed through an exchanger to heat water for dishwashing and cooking.

This is the backstage area at Now and Zen. Like all Zens since his first in Hampstead, ZENW3, the front of house is a performance space where the diners are on display to the street, and the street becomes a stage viewed by the diners. The idea behind these restaurants has always been the same, a trick performed with glass, water, mirrors and light. They are slightly magical places that appear to be much larger than they are, where walls slide away, where structures sometimes seem to defy gravity. But the idea has been refined, Zen by Zen, in a process that parallels what

for Mather amounts to the Holy Grail: the all-glass building. The glazing details on the first Zen are more than satisfactory today by normal standards, but by the standards of Now and Zen, they seem almost crude. And yet Mather is still not entirely satisfied with the minimal metal clamps to the double-height façade glazing at Now and Zen. Bulkier than he wanted, apparently; indeed, he did not want them at all. The glazing, he insists, will hold quite happily on its glued joints alone. Next time...

The Zen saga began, as architectural commissions do, as a chance recommendation from a friend. In 1985 Lawrence Leung, who was establishing a new niche for up-market Chinese food (free of monosodium glutamate, and dubious sweet and sour sauces) and wanted an architectural setting to reflect the quality of the food and the service. The image was to have as little as possible to do with the perceived status of the Chinese restaurant as either a flaky-laminate takeaway or a paper-lanterned Soho den.

The chosen location for the experiment was, appropriately enough, Hampstead – an affluent area of London, with a history of resisting what it sees as an invasion of cheap eateries. It is also a place with a long tradition of resisting innovations in architecture, and then later taking them to its heart. Not far from the proposed Zen, the constructivist architect Erno Goldfinger had built his house, in the teeth of local opposition, in 1938. Hampstead swelled with pride in 1991 when the National Trust adopted Goldfinger's house as its first overtly Modernist property. To open a pioneering restaurant in Hampstead is therefore to have been tested by fire twice over.

The site had been occupied by a down-at-heel vegetarian restaurant half in a listed building, on a corner where a lane leaves Hampstead High Street. When transformed into a Zen, the listed building became effectively an entrance for a Mather glasshouse alongside. There is a double-height glass frontage, and at the rear an angled glass roof for an atrium slot cut down through a mezzanine floor. It became one of the ultimate London dining experiences to mount the stairs with water cascading down one

ZENW3, like the earlier Peter Eaton bookshop, conducts a conversation with the street via double-height glazing. Mather's furniture, first tried at the AA, is developed here

Supporting the slender polished steel handrail at right angles, the staircase baluster (below) acts as a foil to disturbance patterns of the water cascade in the glass trough behind. Overleaf: the first Zen theatre, coming to life after dark

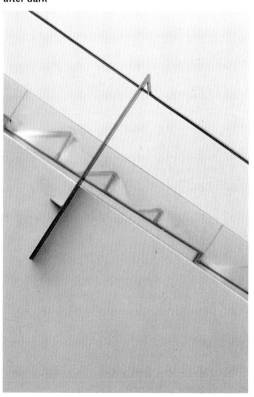

side, cross the bridge across the atrium at the top, and settle down behind the plants in the conservatory to watch the street life. ZENW3 displays in early form all the elements manifested six years later in Now and Zen, not least in its confident sculptural use of space and cutting-away of structure. And it gets away with it in Hampstead, not only by virtue of its cool but confident detailing, but because this is, isn't it, a conservatory. Look, there's a big weeping fig tree inside. People are fond of conservatories in Hampstead.

The photo that went round the world, though, was not any picture of the exterior of ZENW3, or any general shot of the interior, but a particular staircase detail. A slender stainless-steel baluster, at right angles to the slope of the staircase, delicately holds, at a welded junction, a yet more slender rod of a banister rail. Below this, at first glance the edge of the individual stairs are apparent behind obscured glass. However, the stairs appear to be curiously uneven, and surrounded by strange disturbance patterns. This is in fact the edge-on view of what was to become a Zen trademark: the water feature, a symbol of good fortune to the Chinese because the sound of running water represents flowing cash. Here the water cascades down a stepped glass trough at the side of, and some way above, the stairs. At the foot of the stairs, the trough becomes a vertical square glass duct down which the water vanishes. The photograph does not explain this. It is not a photograph of a restaurant at all, or of a building, or of running water, yet it has become a kind of icon of Mather's work.

It shares this with certain other images, such as one of his "house for two psychiatrists" or of the many-bayed window façade at the rear of his 2 Pennington Street office building. These are abstract details plucked out of an overall composition. Naturally, the best architectural photographers (in this case Richard Bryant) are always looking for the striking detail. But within Mather's work, more than most, individual details aspire to the condition of jewellery. For this reason it is slightly shocking, in a Mather building, to encounter seeming crudities, of structure or of finish.

This can be deliberate, as with the exposed sections of oxide-red I-beam in Now and Zen; or they can be due simply to the clumsiness of the building trade, apparent here and there in less than-perfect plastering or joints. Mather's detailing does not easily accommodate slapdash workmanship: he responds well to the work of expert shopfitters such as Pat Carter, who worked for him on two restaurants: Ma and Pa in Whetstone, and Now and Zen in the West End of London.

ZENW3 proved to be a critical success as a restaurant environment. It set the tone for the series that followed: a series of family features emerged, such as the juxtaposition of glass and stainless steel in the elevated bar countertops. The "lucky" water feature became a necessary element of every Zen. Mather's seating designs, for bar stools and chairs, were repeated and refined. And Leung's dictum that there should be no second-rate seat in the house has been scrupulously observed. The idea is that you select your seat according to your own character or mood: some people like to sit in full view of street and fellow diners, others prefer to observe from one side. But no one is, in theatrical terms, stuck behind a pillar.

Mather might be criticised, in his restaurant series that includes the Zens and the spin-off Ma and Pa restaurant in Whetstone, for forging too recognisable an identity. After all, this is now a chain. Should he not have experimented more with different ideas for different Zens?

It is, in truth, a subtle business. A small up-market chain like this, each serving a different clientele, is not exactly Pizza Hut, and does not require that kit-of-parts familiarity. Moreover, the locations do not lend themselves, thankfully, to easy replication. Leung and Mather, for different reasons, both wanted variations on a theme. Mather was refining his ideas, Leung was selling covers. The thing was achieved, perhaps surprisingly, given that the Zens are an exercise in being almost wilfully non-assertive.

Zen Central followed swiftly on the heels of ZENW3. It was not the easiest site to deal with – a redundant post office, a long

Interior by interior, Mather has refined his details, particularly the visual and tactile qualities of steel tube and rod. Zen Central achieved a spidery quality on bar supports (above) to counterpoint the black glass front. Overleaf: at Zen Central, the restaurant is opened up to the street through fold away glass doors for warm weather dining

narrow slot of a space running back from a narrow street frontage. Here, far more than in Hampstead, the need was to create the illusion of space, so from the door, the wall of the restaurant curves round in a sweep to the rear. Kitchens, services and storage are effectively concealed behind this screen, which on the public side defines a circulation area dominated by the black-glass bar, and floored in veined marble. This leaves a long rectangular space, running alongside, that is planned on the existing grid of four equal squares. Each square is defined as a space by one or more devices: flanking columns, a coved ceiling, a circular skylight, or sliding glass partition doors – Zen, like all good Chinese restaurants, likes to have space it can either close off for private parties or open up at times of peak demand.

These squares of space are then doubled in size by running mirror glass down the length of the dining area and across the end wall, and here is where the clever stuff begins. The water feature of Zen Central, for reasons of space as much as anything, was planned to be wall-hung, which meant mounting it on the mirrors. A fearsomely complex system of triangular glass troughs was devised, cascading from level to level down the space. The water flow system had, invisibly, to pass around the structural columns engaged in the wall. The troughs were also internally illuminated. A certain gymnastic ability was required to get all of this to work in the space, and to bring enough light into the rear of the space by means of Mather's trademark circular skylights; here, as at ZENW3 he worked with the young engineer Mark Whitby to achieve the result.

As always, Mather plays games with the lighting: halogen downlighters, defining the edge of the curving wall behind the bar, continue a natural return curve across and into the rear dining area. ZENW3 is still essentially a rectilinear space: the big curve of Zen Central shows the beginning of the subversion of the right angle, a move towards more organic forms, that has become a theme of Mather's later work. Here too, the eminently photographable steel details recur: not just in the elevated glass

Perhaps it should have been a Zen. The life of Fifty-one Fifty-one restaurant at Brompton Cross, complete with Danny Lane fractured glass, was short indeed

countertop, but in some impossibly slender and insect-like supports for glass shelves in the cloakroom. In some respects, it is necessary to use the past tense when speaking of Zen Central. The water cascades were found to require more maintenance than a busy restaurant was prepared to give, and they were eventually replaced by a Danny Lane glass sculpture. Then, in 1991, the restaurant was badly damaged by fire and swiftly restored by the Mather office.

Between Zen Central and Zen Hong Kong, which came in 1988, Mather found himself with a different client for the Fifty-One Fifty-One restaurant at Brompton Cross, rapidly becoming a fashionable quarter of London. It proved to be a short-lived interior, and was totally demolished in 1991, to Mather's disappointment. His reaction to the destruction – an unwillingness to discuss the project as it was when it existed – is indicative of his feelings towards his projects. Looked at objectively, most restaurants are ephemeral pieces of design, victim to changes of fashion and of eating habits. Many interior designers, used to fit-outs destined for only a few years' life, accept the fact and design accordingly. Yet as an architect, Mather does not accept this. His reticent brand of Modernism, coupled with his attention to detail, means that he views these commissions no differently from so-called "permanent" buildings. It sometimes hurts when they go: fortunately for him, relatively few have so far bitten the dust.

Other projects ran concurrently with the Zen series, among them what turned out to be the difficult commission for Point West, an apartment block created out of the hulk of the former West London Air Terminal on Cromwell Road. Another house, in Belgravia, and a major remodelling job for the Waddington Galleries in Cork Street, passed through the office. Then came the Hong Kong Zen, a coals-to-Newcastle commission that is one of the most satisfying in the series.

Here, Mather was not faced with the prospect of transforming an unpromising and awkward bit of traditional city space. Zen Hong Kong is in Pacific Place, a vast complex of shops, offices, hotels, apartments put together by one of the colony's great trading groups, Swires. Indeed, forty floors of hotel tower rise above the Zen slot on the shopping mall. It is intensely public at a point where the crowds debouch from lifts and escalators. But for all the intense competition from a myriad other restaurants, some within the shopping centre itself, Zen Hong Kong had a peculiarity which for Mather was another odd "first": this was the first Chinese restaurant to be designed by a non-Chinese in the city. Like designing the first new antiquarian bookshop in London for 50 years, it was a strange distinction to achieve, but a highly visible one.

As Mather later found with Now and Zen in London, to take a slot in a new development earmarked for a restaurant is by no means the easy option it might appear to be. Seemingly "difficult" sites may offer more than the ready-provided space. At Pacific Place, the given space was, however, gratifyingly weird: roughly triangular in plan, with great fat columns crashing down into it from the hotel tower up above, and some cyclopean and very rough concrete beams spanning overhead. This suited Mather's increasing dislike of the simple rectangle, a factor which by chance coincided in certain respects with Chinese Fung Shui observance, which prefers diagonal planning (Norman Foster had earlier consulted the Fung Shui geomancer Koo Pak Ling over the planning of his nearby Hong Kong and Shanghai Bank – one reason for its offset escalators, apart from anything else). However, the big problem remained the ceiling. What to do with those great beams? Hide them behind a suspended ceiling? Render them up and paint them? In the end, Mather decided to leave them just as they were, in their raw state. Lights and air-conditioning ducts are carefully placed between them.

From the mall, the façade appears as an undulating glass front, rising from a plinth of polished black granite to a straightforward white ceiling above: a ceiling that gives way beyond the window zone to the brute concrete of the structure. There is in Zen philosophy the notion of the beneficial effect

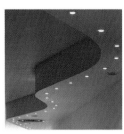

The slightly 1930s feel of intersecting planes in the constricted frontage of Ma and Pa restaurant (above) continues in the sculpted ceiling (right) and glass water cascade (below). Opposite: the "water dragon" at Zen HK

of a contrast of opposites. Even so, the contrast between the considered, fine-line detail of Mather's work – more Japanese than Chinese – and the rough mass of the exposed structure is something of a shock.

The sinusoidal glass wall was to recur in later projects, notably Mather's 2 Pennington Street office block in London, but here its form is echoed in the "water dragon" feature, an undulating series of suspended shallow glass bowls, where water trickles from one to the other, running right through the centre of the space. Doubly lucky, this: not only the luck of running water, but the luck of the dragon as well.

There are few concessions to Chinese materials or ornament in Zen Hong Kong: the same whites, greys and blacks are used, and no one has ever claimed that a Le Corbusier Grand Confort armchair has oriental overtones. Yet for his walls, Mather here chose a zebrawood panelling, again disposed on the diagonal, that gives a big-scale pattern and a warmer feel. Otherwise, the main Zen attributes are there, in particular the notion of the diner as both performer and spectator. There are few more public spaces to sit than just inside the wavy wall looking on to the mall of Pacific Place.

Having made it in Hong Kong, Mather could lay claim to one of those slightly bizarre architectural singularities: to be the Western architect with the best understanding of the art and craft of Chinese restaurants. Although the Zens continued – Leung is nothing if not a loyal client – Mather has not become trapped in a role which has dogged several talented architects of the 1980s: of being typecast as a modish café and restaurant architect. Ma and Pa, the Chinese restaurant in Whetstone for Eric Ma, a former member of the Leung empire, was completed in 1989, but by then other projects, such as the development plan for the University of East Anglia at Norwich and a study for a station and shopping complex at South Quay on the Docklands Light Railway, were under way.

Ma and Pa has elements both of Now and Zen and Pennington

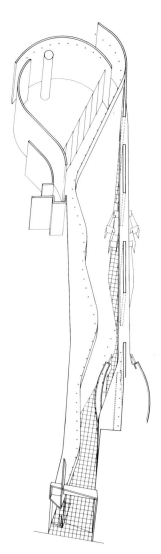

From a 3.5m wide street frontage, Ma and Pa extends back 45m. The curves of the restaurant terminate behind the translucent glass screen of the private dining room

Street about it. Stylistically, it is a Zen in everything but name, right down to the furniture. Mather's interest in using air-conditioning ducting to help sculpt the ceiling plane is apparent, so is his desire to, in his favourite phrase, "give something to the street". Difficult, here. The restaurant space is very deep but narrows at the entrance to a ridiculous slot of 3 × 3.5 metres, surrounded by suburban tat shopfronts. The need, then, was to signal the restaurant vigorously while at the same time eschewing the Las Vegas strip approach normally adopted in such situations. As at Pennington Street, this is done by leaning a little of the frontage forward, in this case like a rectilinear hood. Set off by a heroic vertical fin and washed with light, the frontage attracts attention purely as an abstract composition. Once drawn there like a moth to a lamp, the view is into seductive mirrored and glass-divided spaces, complete with a water cascade of intersecting planes worthy of Rietveld. It is a glacial kind of place in the context of snooker clubs and pizza takeaways – not for the faint-hearted window-shopping for food.

The spatial experiments of the restaurants were beginning to attract notice and pay off in more mainstream commissions: larger projects such as the student residences at UEA, and the Pennington Street office building. But the Zens continued. Zen Montreal, in 1990, was typical Mather territory: a dark basement (formerly a Post-modern nightclub) beneath the city's Four Seasons Hotel which he zipped open and lit up with a confidence now born of experience. The lighting and ceiling moulding in Montreal is getting very sophisticated. The sinusoidal wall is there, internal and plastered rather than the glass of Hong Kong. Mather's increasing fascination with solid colour to act as a foil to all that icy transparency – evident to some extent in Ma and Pa – starts to show up strongly as well. The wavy wall is bright yellow. Greenish glass strip tiles clad the bar podium. Polished black granite, as in Hong Kong, encircles it. The plan is of a sequence of spirals, which serves naturally to create separated eating areas while moving towards more fluid, organic forms. The twinkling halogen spots in the ceiling have that slightly random placing that hints at constellations.

It was appropriate, then, that when another Zen was proposed for London, it should be in Orion House, the Po-mo'd early 1960s building in St Martin's Lane – theatreland – that gave Mather the excuse for a visual pun (subtler than the catchy name, Now and Zen). A curious little cluster of spotlights on the ceiling of the upper floor, arranged for no apparent purpose, may be recognised by those astronomers among the clientèle as the shape of the constellation Orion. As at Hong Kong, this was a space in a commercial development specifically intended for a restaurant. Also as in Hong Kong, the space – effectively a single floor with awkward level changes and no natural lighting at the rear – was anything but ideal for Mather's purposes. Some structural gymnastics were needed to insert the mezzanine and make the spaces work: the engineer was Tim MacFarlane. The overall lighting here comes from a variety of sources: wall- and ceiling-mounted halogen spots, concealed lighting in the sculpted coves of the ceilings, low-wattage tungsten fittings at foot level (of the unbreakable glass variety normally found in ovens) to illuminate the stairs. The lighting at Now and Zen was Mather's subtlest and most effective to date.

What strikes you about Now and Zen is not at first the lighting, which is intended to go virtually unnoticed, but Mather's most radical "lucky water" feature to date. Derived from the glass-bowl dragon in Zen Hong Kong, this is much refined – the bowls almost seeming to defy gravity as they swoop in a great spiral from the mezzanine to the ground floor to the basement, reflected, of course, in mirrors to increase the apparent length of the chain. The stainless-steel structure that supports and braces the bowls in their descent is a very spidery structural arrangement of steel and glass. They seem impossibly fragile: Mather tried out four prototype versions in his office to make sure it would work. It does. He is given to worrying the restaurant staff by leaning over the mezzanine, seizing one of the steel cord

The vertical strip tiling
in the bar counter at
Zen Montreal (right) was
to become a recurrent
device: translated to
Roman brick, it later
clad a key elevation
of Mather's Pennington
Street office building.
Below: detail of the glass
feature on the ground
floor. Angled cool sheets
of glass are arranged in
iceberg formation
around the balustrade,
defining the space
on this level

Refinement of detail: Now and Zen's cascading glass-bowl water feature (top) and entrance (above), with a specially designed all-glass revolving door inset into a taut glass skin above a glass floor

hangers and shaking the whole snake vigorously to demonstrate how it returns naturally to its designed position. The staff in turn like to tell the customers that the flow of water from bowl to bowl increases when it is raining outside.

The snake of bowls has the effect of tying together all three levels of eating: an important matter when your client's philosophy is to have no bad seats. Although the mezzanine level with its skeletal nautical balustrading is one obvious place to be, and the ground-level diners can gaze just as directly out into the street, it is the basement area that shows this philosophy at its strongest. There cannot be any horizontal views out here: a condition that is ameliorated by Mather's reinterpretation of the old trick of pavement lights. This is turned into a solid glass ceiling to the street itself, a ceiling that you have already walked across, via a slate-paved bridge, when you entered the restaurant through its (all glass) revolving door. But the gangplank is there more for reassurance than anything: the glass is strong enough, being supported at intervals on pared-down steel T-beams, not only to take the weight of people, but cars as well. A runaway taxi careering down St Martin's Lane ought not to come crashing though on to the diners below.

The glass ceiling device gives the basement some connection with the street – a perpetual Mather concern. It is then connected back to the life of the rest of the restaurant by the ox-eye hole cut in the floor slab above, with the trickling water bowls spiralling down through. The effect of the aperture is of a kind of vortex through which space and light are funnelled.

Public though dining is here – the taut skin of the full-height entrance glazing, bonded with glue, clamped with minimal stainless-steel fixings and incorporating a revolving door that is all glass apart from its pintle bearings and edge brushes – it is a restaurant where access from one level to another is concealed. The stairs from level to level are relatively narrow and steep, relatively dark, and so make the emergence into the various spaces more of an occasion. Those spaces are terminated at the rear by the most perfectly finished and complete mirror elevations that Mather had yet installed. You really are fooled into thinking that the restaurant is twice the size it is: a device that works best on the mezzanine level, where the stainless-steel balustrading extends right up to the glass.

Mather shows an increasing confidence with colour at Now and Zen. Exposed steel is blood-red, not only in expressed columns but in the short length of I-beam connecting the edge of the curving mezzanine level with the crosswall, which some have read as a slightly lewd protruding tongue. The colour recurs on the edges of the folded steel stairs, left standing proud. The rear wall is bright yellow, Lutyens yellow: a concrete column that rises through all three floors is (Western) imperial purple. Carpets are Mather's favourite bluish-green, used on all Zens except the first two with their chopstick pattern carpeting, and are here related to the colour of the edge of the glass bowls and the glass-strip mosaic cladding the bar. As a result, and unlike Mather's previous restaurants, the view into Now and Zen at night is one of colour, (appropriate for a site in the centre of London's theatreland) contrasted with fine stainless-steel details. For this Zen, Mather redesigned his family of furniture to use much narrower-gauge metal in a far more complex way. Mather's latest bar stools are a virtual exercise in constructivism, and a further declaration of intention to refine details to their utmost.

Do mere restaurants deserve such design attention? Do diners appreciate it? Will clients preserve it? Is it not a talent wasted that could be better used elsewhere? For Mather, who is if anything over-protective of his restaurant spaces, the experience with Zen has enabled him to develop a coherent and elegant vocabulary, applicable to projects on almost any scale, in almost any variety of space. It is like the artist obsessively working over and over again the same scene. There is therefore a lot of Zen in the big Pennington Street building, which would have been a great deal less rich without its small-scale restaurant predecessors.

An axonometric of
Now and Zen showing
the various levels and
elements of the design,
from the glass water
feature, which runs
from the highest point
in the ceiling, over
the mezzanine balcony
through the circular
space down to the
ground and basement
floors, to the all-glass
revolving door

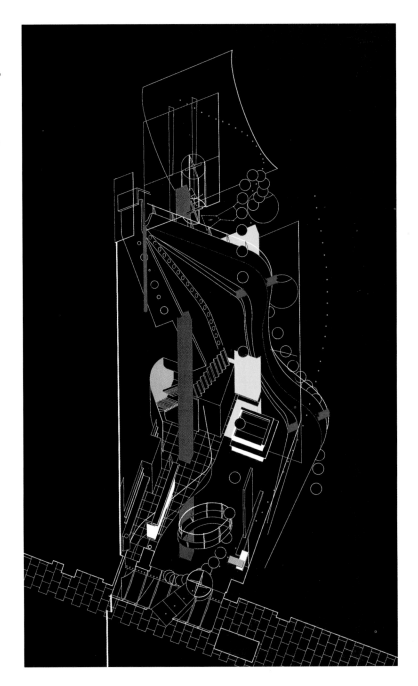

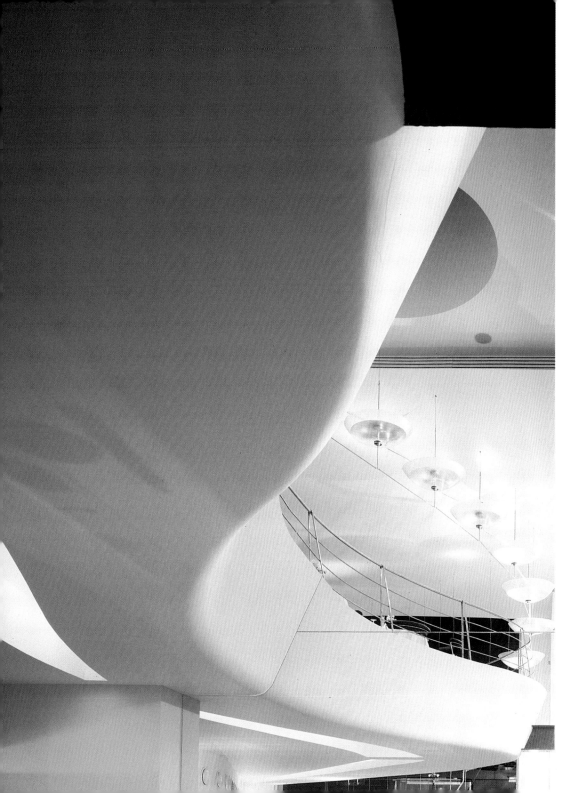

The downstairs eating area at **Now** and **Zen** is linked to the upper floors by use of colour as well as the gurgling snake of water bowls

LANDMARK FOR THE CITY

Previous pages: the
Pennington Street office
building, later named
"La Lumière" by its
owner, brought Mather
to public attention
as never before through
his fresh handling of
large-scale elevations

The quietly gleeful side of Rick Mather's nature is not immediately obvious. A disciplined, controlled type, he is far more likely to fret over details than to enthuse about the overall effect. But he is very sure of himself. One day, gazing at his Pennington Street office block, he remarked: "The one thing I'm pleased about is that this is an interesting building. We've actually managed to make it work." This, decoded, is a ringing self-endorsement along the lines of Erno Goldfinger's reported response to one of his own buildings: "You have to admit, it really is very good." What Pennington Street manages to work out is a way of handling a big elevation with complete confidence in a modern manner. This was the biggest project Mather had undertaken to date, and the first on this large scale since his mid-eighties UEA buildings had adopted some of the devices of classicism for the façades.

Pennington Street, which brought Mather to his widest audience yet, only really came about because of another large-scale exercise – a commission that turned out to be rather less satisfactory. The developer Berkley House had taken on the former West London Air Terminal in the Cromwell Road with the intention of converting this 1960s administration building into apartments. The attraction was its height: by keeping within the envelope of the existing structure, a massively greater density of housing could be achieved than would be allowed on a cleared site.

Mather entered a slightly confused situation in 1987. His old friend Michael Baumgarten, who was later to bring him the Pennington Street job, was involved in the scheme, known as Point West. Baumgarten had previously worked with Julyan Wickham on another Berkley House project, Horselydown Square by Tower Bridge. When Baumgarten split from Wickham to set up his development consultancy, he was taken on by Berkley House to sort out Point West. In-house architects were working on the complex and Baumgarten called in Mather to suggest a location for a restaurant in the foot of the tower.

The foot of the West London Air Terminal was one of the worst urban spaces imaginable. Away from the road, with a Sainsbury's

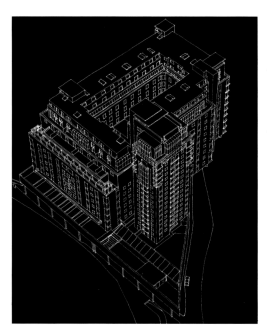

Point West was an exercise in making the best of an awkward job at the behest of architect-developer Michael Baumgarten. Mather conjured a large-scale apartment block out of a 1960s office slab

supermarket taking up most of the available ground-level space, the site did not even have a front door. The way in, other architects had decided, was through the supermarket service yard via a lane running along the railway tracks at the rear – scarcely inspiring.

Encouraged by Baumgarten, Mather took the plans home and re-designed the base of the tower over the weekend, giving it a front door that allowed direct access through to the Cromwell Road. Baumgarten liked the possibilities that the new approach opened up and asked Mather to cast an eye over the façade treatment. Not only was it in lumpen Po-mo style with giant granite ribbons and roundels that Mather describes as "thumb tacks", but it also featured over a thousand different window types. This was more than a weekend job: the window types were reduced to a basic three and the elevational treatment was simplified into plainer, lightly modelled brick façades.

Mather soon found himself redesigning the entire exterior, element by element. It was not exactly a dream job, but it was large and it had one big plus: a three-floor penthouse on top of the tower. Commanding enviable views over West London, Mather slimmed down the penthouse into a kind of conning tower to give something of a 1930s, Joseph Emberton, feel. He added a two-storey high conservatory, an indoor swimming pool with portholes to look out over London from under water, and a roof garden placed just as high as it was possible to go, 18 floors up. This was the most ambitious example yet of the celebrated Mather upside-down house principle in action.

Mather's drawings were then handed over to the supervising architects. Although Baumgarten kept him involved, the details inevitably ended up coarser than Mather intended. More worrying were the difficulties the developer was getting into. Much of the structural frame of the terminal building needed rebuilding and credit had to be extended right at the bottom of the recession, at a time when few people were looking for costly sky-rise apartments. Eventually, with the creditors owing large sums of money, the project was forced into receivership. Work stopped just before the

Designed to anchor the eastern fringes of the City of London financial district, the Pennington Street block announces itself to the passing motorist with some of the bold devices of pre-war Modernism, most notably the punctured roof canopy and leaning glass totem (left). More apparent to the pedestrian is the ground-level sinusoidal glass wall (right) that Mather first used in Zen Hong Kong

building's completion, and was only resumed some time later, by a different developer. In 1991, Mather summed up the episode briefly: "The design is much better than when we first got involved," he remarked, "and the building does now have a front door."

Pennington Street had none of the urbanistic problems of Point West. It's right on the street – but what a street. Mather had to find a way to signal the building's presence on The Highway, the arterial road running east from the City of London to Docklands, at one of the few points where traffic can speed between the traffic jams at each end. Baumgarten, here freed from the shackles of conventional developers and in a key role, made it clear from the start that Pennington Street, a speculative office block in a fringe location, had to advertise itself. He went further: when the stack of site huts was erected at the front of the cleared site, he hid them behind a hoarding depicting Mather's own slightly preppy features in anamorphic form which read correctly from the angle of approaching vehicles. When the building was completed, Mather's staff secretly rescued the big-brotherish hoarding and carefully re-erected it in the car park behind his Camden office.

Given that the site was formerly a decaying complex of sheds and wine warehouses, and that other new insertions in this length of street have adopted the usual ersatz warehouse mode, it would have been simple to conform. Indeed there was an existing, far more expensive but nonetheless anodyne scheme with planning permission for the site which could have been built straight off, but Baumgarten did not want to fall into line.

Baumgarten, who died tragically and unexpectedly while the building was near completion in 1991, was in the business of niche-marketing: selling sophisticated design at relatively low rents in off-pitch locations. He had changed his mind about what he wanted several times during the short gestation and construction period of the 11,200-square-metre building – for the most part, changes prompted by shifts in the nature of the commercial property market. But Baumgarten knew what architecture was about and, as an accomplished joiner, knew the importance of

Mather's own profile, used anamorphically, decorates the site hoarding at Pennington Street and publicises a design-conscious development

     Rick Mather: Urban Approaches

good detailing. So although this was to be a design-and-build contract, Mather's office retained a high degree of supervision.

The brief was for a pitched-roof building, which allowed for the butterfly roof option, a device also by this time exploited with success by Norman Foster in his low-cost office building at Stockley Park. As at UEA, the need was to increase the apparent scale where the building faced north on to The Highway, to allow concealed skylights for the deep plan, and to hide the roof plant. Also, for the fun of it, by pulling the shiny white soffit of the roof out over a top-level balcony and then perforating it with ten large holes, the effect is again of pre-war heroic Modernism; as Professor Colquhoun has pointed out, also a possible reference to New York's Museum of Modern Art. There are other references: as with Emberton's Simpson's department store in the Strand of 1935, the device gives a scale to the top of the building and has the aesthetic advantage of removing the need for rainwater downpipes on the key elevation.

The second device to add scale here is a full-height strip of opaque Planar glass, held in tension some ten degrees out from the face of the building at the top, where it projects through a square aperture in the roof edge and runs down in front of the lower balconied floors to just above the entrance canopy. This is, really, an illuminated sign (back-lit at night), even though it carries no words or logos. It's original rationale was to protect an open escape stair, and was retained as part of the composition when, later, the district surveyor insisted on the escape stair being enclosed within the envelope of the building. Wanting the leaning sentry apparently to defy gravity still more, Mather originally intended that it should be constructed of glass blocks, bonded and held invisibly by a concealed stainless-steel frame. However, the testing procedure could not meet the critical path of the construction programme – there was not enough time.

The leaning soldier of glass links the equally powerful horizontal elements at the top and base of the building: an undulating floor-to-ceiling wall of glass at street level which catches the light as you flash past, and above which the masonry rectangle of the façade appears to float. The columns on this north façade, standing clear of the building's skin at the eastern end, provide the additional big vertical scale that the site demands. These are the elements that register the building on the retina at 50 miles per hour, the average speed of traffic along this part of the road. The upwards tilt of the roof is enough to catch the sun as it moves round the sky to the south, enlivening a northern façade which is otherwise in shadow for most of the day. Sunlight is also captured by roof-lights on the top floor and brought directly inside.

At walking rather than driving speed, the subtler details of the north façade become apparent. The Roman brick elevation is not square to the site, but is almost imperceptibly cranked in order to join flush with the buildings on either side. This means that its order of columns, the expressed concrete frame of the building which is square, emerges from the façade as your eye travels from west to east. A simple, single-storey column at the western end becomes full-height at the east, the beams of the building's frame breaking through the brickwork to meet it.

A pattern of both square and rectangular windows is punched through the brick "bookends" of the façade, and punched brick continues across at first floor level to express the angled surface connecting the two adjacent building façades. But the central fully-glazed portion with its balconies is orthogonal to the columns, not the brickwork, so it appears slightly skewed, like a movable element, a drawer pushed in at an angle. The top balcony, clad in Roman brick but also square with the columns, is therefore not cranked like the first floor, but runs straight along the top, parting company with the lower courses until a return at the eastern end.

The sinusoidal glass wall at ground level is a token of Mather's perpetual attempt to bring the life of the building close to the life of the street. The device, which he first used in Zen Hong Kong, is used here as a way to overcome the obstacle of smoke vents from the basement car-park below. Instead of the usual set-back from the street, the billowing glass, coming out almost to kiss the

Reflection on the
courtyard walls of
Pennington Street –
gantry bridges
connect the ends of
the two wings

Landmark for the City

Pennington Street's
north face (below), on
The Highway – the need
was to increase the
apparent scale. The plan
(bottom left) shows
how the depth of the
site is exploited

The top-floor balcony
(opposite) with a pierced
canopy reminiscent of
MOMA, looks across at
the City of London

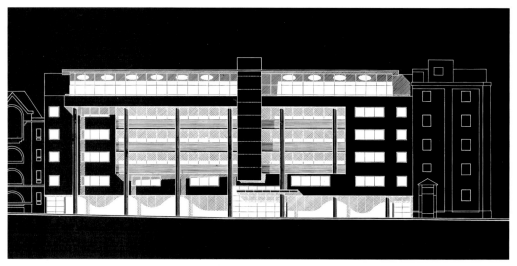

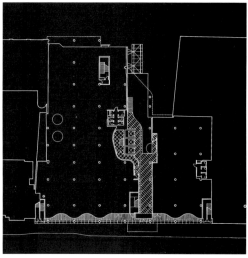

Rick Mather: Urban Approaches

The curving wall of
Pennington Street's
southern setback
(opposite) leads to
a stack of walkways
linking lift lobbies
with the western office
wing. They will
provide a green wall
of trailing plants

column line before swooping back in again, engages with the
street while still allowing room for the vents. The Mannerist gesture
therefore has a Functionalist rationale, not to mention a
commercial reality: the aim is to attract attention to space that
could well be let as shops, a showroom, or a restaurant. The wavy
wall reads well on the oblique views you get along the street.

Though he worked the main façade hard to create a forceful
impression on The Highway, Mather reined back just as hard on
the rear elevation, on Pennington Street itself. The street is a
strange one – a narrow service road of tarmac-patched granite
setts running along the quarter-mile blind wall of an 1804 rum
warehouse – now housing Times Newspapers, part of the News
International empire. It continues east to Tobacco Dock, a Georgian
proto-high-tech warehouse complex now converted by Terry Farrell
into a speciality shopping centre. The northern side of the street
is a collection of junk buildings, many formerly light industrial
spaces and garages. The street and these buildings suggest one
scale; the looming bulk of Rupert Murdoch's News International
plant, rising behind, suggests another.

Mather pitched it somewhere in between. The need for a big
set-back to allow daylight to a residential warehouse conversion
alongside presented the possibility of a landscaped courtyard
that is also the granite-paved entrance to the basement car park,
although this function is played down. The set-back is achieved
with a wall that gently curves round from the lightwell at the centre
of the building to a 45-degree angle, cutting across to the lower
entrance with its steel and glass canopy. Two rectilinear volumes
are slid out beneath the angled wall at right angles to each other:
the glass entrance lobby, and the slate-clad form of the ground-
floor showroom. The angled wall, its Roman bricks set vertically
to emphasise the curve, is pierced with triangular bay windows,
aligned with the structural grid of the building and glazed all
round: it is possible to look vertically downwards, upwards or
due south, but the west-facing pane is opaque because it faces
the windows of the adjacent flats.

On a smaller scale, two of the elements of the main north elevation are repeated: the perforated oversailing roof canopy, and the obscured glass staircase marker, here weathertight and rather more functional, but set vertically so as not to overwhelm the narrow street. From the rear entrance it is possible to see right through the building, up a level and out the front to the trees on the other side of The Highway, this despite the depth of the building plot. Indeed, the quiet neighbourliness of the deeply-modelled back elevation with all its constraints offers more to the eye than the heroism of the front. Its intersecting geometries have more in common with the vertical section of Mather's houses and restaurants.

The building as a whole provides a wide open L-shaped rectangular office floorplate at the front, linked via a one-bay width office "bridge" to a rough parallelogram of a floorplan at the rear. Gantry bridges across the rear courtyard connect the ends of the two wings and are wide enough to carry planting boxes. A service core of lifts and glass-block stairs descends through the central lightwell, at the foot of which, spanned by the office bridge, is some thoughtful landscaping by Georgie Wolton. The extremely sheltered conditions allowed semi-hardy species to be introduced despite the fact that there is no conventionally glazed atrium roof.

This aspect was one of the keys to the early design of the building. Having an open lightwell rather than an atrium meant that the floors could be naturally cross-ventilated rather than air-conditioned. Later, when pension funds ceased to invest in office buildings unless they had full air-conditioning (whether it was needed or not), the building was duly air-conditioned: Mather had to thicken the raised floor, but the room proportions fortunately were robust enough to take it. The system chosen is controllable zone by zone, in the hope that future occupants of the building will realise that they don't actually need to turn it on.

Inside, there are references to other Mather jobs: pink/gold glass mosaic in the lift lobbies, for instance, is the same as that used on the bar at the Ma and Pa restaurant, while the use of glass block for the stairwell finds echoes in many other projects. The high standard of wood finish in the prefabricated lavatory pods are also redolent of the restaurant rather than the office block. Slender Roman brick was chosen not just for its proportions and ochre colour but also for its dense, readily-cleaned texture.

At Pennington Street, all the elements came together in what was, for Mather, his most significant project to date. Variously pigeon-holed at one time or another as a teaching architect, a house-conversion architect, or a restaurant-and-bars architect, here he was designing 11,200-square-metre prime City floorspace for an avant-garde developer. With this building he had joined a vigorous tributary of the commercial mainstream at the same time that his public-sector educational work was expanding, at UEA and with a new masterplanning commission for part of Imperial College in London focusing on Princes Gardens. Mather is still working on domestic jobs, producing an extension to a house in Hampstead which pursues his fascination with the structural properties of glass – an entirely crystalline structure.

In 1992, the practice won a limited competition for new student residences at Keble College, Oxford. Three sites were identified within the existing network of venerable and distinguished buildings where new development could take place to increase accommodation to an optimum size. The first space, at the end of the Fellow's Garden, was adjacent to one of the college's original premises, designed by William Butterfield. Set in an extremely sensitive location, the new residence building, although modern, was carefully designed to tie in to the existing context. Its height and material would be similar to the surrounding nineteenth-century buildings; placing the residence on the edge of the garden left the maximum usable free space in the middle, and left a number of huge ancient plane trees undisturbed.

Drawing on experience gained at UEA, the accommodation itself was designed to very high standards of finish and was environmentally responsible. Super insulation and heat recovery reduces energy consumption such that central heating is not

The north façade of Pennington Street, (right), is a deceptively complex, deeply modelled affair. The elevation cranks slightly from west to east in varying planes, the building's frame emerging as a column order. On the south elevation (opposite), triangular bay windows pierce the Roman brick wall which gently curves at 45 degrees from the central lightwell

Rick Mather: Urban Approaches

The small house extension (opposite) signalled a return to a particular Mather enthusiasm – the structural properties of glass. This is an all-glass building. Below: a preliminary drawing for new student residences at Keble College, Oxford – designed to fit into the existing context of venerable and distinguished buildings

required and all building materials and appliances were evaluated on the basis of the energy used to produce and run them.

The completions of Now and Zen and Pennington Street once again raised the question of Mather's style, which had, without a doubt, changed tack since the UEA buildings of a few years before. If, as he said then, he was schooled in the discipline of Modernism, then what kind of Modernism had it become? Mather is anything but faddish, but is not immune to changing fashions. The classical devices of the early UEA work is right for the time; the spirit of a certain kind of pre-war Modernism, apparent in his latest work, is a response to the different enthusiasms of the 1990s, a desire for a style beyond function.

Mather takes the line – agreeing with Colin Rowe and others – that in any event much of modern architecture is closely akin to Mannerism. He regards narrow Functionalism as limiting and silly, certainly un-architectural. "I'd consider it a compliment to be called a Mannerist," Mather states. "After all Michelangelo started it – and he's one of the greats if not the greatest." Whatever the influence or the enthusiasm, there is a clearer line to be discerned running through the work of Mather than there is in that of many architects. A particular concern has always been apparent in his oeuvre, from the first timber house in Oregon: a desire to work with, rather than against, the context. A house is built to peer over the trees; a restaurant interior is designed to become part of the street; an office building is scaled to read from the traffic corridor. It has always been an essentially urban and urbanising approach.

In 1989 the office moved out of Primrose Gardens to the roomier upper floor of a former billiard hall, right in the heart of the urban tangle of Camden Town. Mather had finally separated home and office completely. With the big interventions at UEA scheduled for completion in the twentieth anniversary year of his setting up in pratice back in Arlington Road, Mather had by imperceptible degrees got to the point of being recognised as an important figure in British architecture. The funny thing was this: to the outside world it seemed as if he had arrived overnight.

Rick Mather: Urban Approaches

Selected chronology and project credits

- Student residences, Keble College, Oxford
  Team: Rick Mather, Glyn Emrys, Roberto Pascual Spada,
  Dusan Decermic (commissioned 1992)

- Student residences, University of East Anglia, Norwich
  Team: Rick Mather, Douglas McIntosh, Glyn Emrys,
  Roberto Pascual Spada, James Slade, Dusan Decermic,
  John Cockings, Mark Annen, Michael Delaney,
  Chris Procter, Charles Barclay, Voon Wong, Chris Bagot
  (commissioned 1989)

- UEA Drama Studio, University of East Anglia, Norwich
  Team: Rick Mather, Ian Hay, Michael Foster,
  (commissioned 1991)

- Remodelling of penthouse flat, Neal's Yard, London
  Client: Nick Stolberg
  Team: Rick Mather, Charles Barclay (commissioned 1991)

● 1991
All-glass extension, Hampstead, London
Client: Sir Leonard and Lady Hoffmann
Team: Rick Mather, Timothy Dodd, Ian Hay

● 1991
Pennington Street office building, Wapping, London
Client: Calderford Limited – M J Gleeson Group Plc
Team: Rick Mather, Glyn Emrys, Pascal Madoc Jones,
Douglas McIntosh, John Cockings, Thomas Deckker,
Thomas Verebes

● 1991
Redevelopment proposal for student residences,
conference centre, health club and restaurants, Imperial
College of Science, Technology & Medicine, London
Team: Rick Mather, Pascal Madoc Jones,
Christopher Mascall, Russell Jones

● 1991
Now and Zen restaurant, Upper St Martins Lane,
London
Client: Blaidwood Limited
Team: Rick Mather, Ian Hay, Timothy Dodd, Glyn Emrys,
Dusan Decermic, John Cockings, Rebekah Staveley,
Michael Delaney, Mark Annen

● 1990
Winning proposal – restaurant complex, Millwall Dock,
London
Client: London Docklands Development Corporation
Team: Rick Mather, Ian Hay, Douglas McIntosh,
Dusan Decermic, Thomas Verebes

● 1990
Zen restaurant, Four Seasons hotel, Montreal
Client: Blaidwood Limited
Team: Rick Mather, Ian Hay, Graham Livesey,
Dusan Decermic, Guillermo Millacet

● 1989
Zen restaurant, Pacific Place, Hong Kong
Client: Blaidwood Limited
Team: Rick Mather, Pascal Madoc Jones,
Douglas McIntosh

● 1989
Ma and Pa restaurant, Whetstone, London
Client: Eric Ma
Team: Rick Mather, Ian Hay

● 1989
Private residence, Belgravia, London
Client: Professor and Mrs Ronald Dworkin
Team: Rick Mather, Stephen Archer, Thomas Croft,
Dusan Decermic

● 1988
25-year campus development plan
Client: University of East Anglia, Norwich
Team: Rick Mather, Douglas McIntosh, Mark Annen,
Stephen Keyser

● 1988
Point West, South Kensington, London
Client: Berkley House and Land Investors
Team: Rick Mather, Glyn Emrys, David Naessens,
Stephen Keyser, Dan Naegele, Charles Emberson,
Antoinette O'Neal, Ian Montgomerie

● 1988
South Quay Light Rail station proposal, Isle of Dogs,
London
Client: London Docklands Development Corporation
Team: Rick Mather, Douglas McIntosh, Stephen Keyser

● **1988**
Art gallery, Mayfair, London
Client: Waddington Galleries Limited
Team: Rick Mather, Thomas Croft, Stephen Archer

● **1988**
Fifty-One Fifty-One restaurant, Brompton Cross, London
Client: Robert Earl
Team: Rick Mather, Carolyn Trevor, Pascal Madoc Jones

● **1987**
Zen Central restaurant, Mayfair, London
Client: Blaidwood Limited
Team: Rick Mather, Pascal Madoc Jones

● **1986**
Studio residence and art gallery, Belsize Park, London
Client: Margaret Lipworth
Team: Rick Mather, Thomas Croft, David Naessens,
Stephen Archer

● **1986**
ZENW3 restaurant, Hampstead, London
Client: Blaidwood Limited
Team: Rick Mather, Pascal Madoc Jones

● **1986**
Residential complex, Bermondsey, London
Client: Courtbeam Limited
Team: Rick Mather, Bill Greensmith, Mark Guard,
Thomas Croft

● **1985**
Climatic Research Unit building
Client: University of East Anglia, Norwich
Team: Rick Mather, Mark Guard, Bill Greensmith,
Jim Conti, David Naessens

● **1984**
Schools of Education and Information Systems building
Client: University of East Anglia, Norwich
Team: Rick Mather, Bill Greensmith, Mark Guard,
Jim Conti, David Naessens

● **1984**
Architectural Association, Bedford Square, London
Team: Rick Mather, Penny Richards, David Selby,
Neil Morton

● **1982**
Residential compound and water garden,
Khartoum, Sudan
Client: Sutrac
Team: Rick Mather, Penny Richards, Jim Conti,
David Naessens, Ian Hay

● **1981**
Psychiatrist's residence and offices, Chalk Farm, London
Client: Dr and Mrs William Gillespie
Team: Rick Mather, Bill Greensmith

● **1979**
Artist's residence and studio, Kentish Town, London
Client: Guy Gladwell
Team: Rick Mather, Derek Tynan, Neil Morton

● **1978**
Architect's residence and offices, Belsize Park, London
Client: Rick Mather
Team: Rick Mather, Derek Tynan, Mark Gregg

● **1975**
Peter Eaton bookshop, Holland Park, London
Client: Peter Eaton Antiquarian Booksellers Limited
Team: Rick Mather, Peter Roy, John Parker,
Andrew Goodenough

● **1972**
Architect's residence and offices, Camden Town,
London
Client: Rick Mather
Architect: Rick Mather

Selected chronology and project credits

● **UK consultants include**
  Quantity surveyors: Peter Henderson Associates,
  Stockings & Clarke, Hanscomb,
  Davis Langdon & Everest
  Structural engineers: Dewhurst Macfarlane Partnership,
  Whitby & Bird, Jenkins & Potter,
  Alan Baxter & Associates, Barton Wells, Price & Myers,
  Vincent Grant Partnership
  Service consultants: Fulcrum Engineering,
  Paul Ruyssevelt, Helix, FISEC, Isometrix
  Planning consultant: Trevor Hollinger
  Landscaping consultant: Georgie Wolton

● **UK contractors include**
  Pat Carter Shopfitting, R G Carter Ltd, Finetimber Ltd,
  M J Gleeson Group Plc, William H Green & Sons,
  Martin Spacey, Wates (East) Construction

● **Administration staff**
  Edward van Finnamore, Elena Acciarri, Aya Ruppin